FRIENDSHIP TOWARDS PEACE

For Barbara,
who showed me in many ways
that friendship between two people
can be a blessing to others

Ronald A. Wells

Friendship towards Peace

THE JOURNEY OF KEN NEWELL AND GERRY REYNOLDS

the columba press

First published in 2005 by
the columba press
55A Spruce Avenue, Stillorgan Industrial Park,
Blackrock, Co Dublin

Cover by Bill Bolger
Origination by The Columba Press
Printed in Ireland by ColourBooks Ltd, Dublin

ISBN 1 85607 475 7

Table of Contents

Preface

Peacemakers in Northern Ireland will know why we chose the title for this book. People from the two main faith communities have only seldom been friends. Moreover, leaders from Protestant and Catholic sides of the divided society would hardly ever refer to a person from the other side as a best friend. On one level, it is a small enough thing to have a best friend; in this context, however, it is remarkable. It is that remarkable story we have to tell in this book. The main actors in the story – Fr Gerry Reynolds and Rev Ken Newell – have a personal friendship that has had huge public implications about what it means to be a Christian in Northern Ireland. The two friends have motivated many people from their respective communities of origin to join them on the journey towards peace and reconciliation.

Six years ago I published a book, *People Behind the Peace: Community and Reconciliation in Northern Ireland,* in which I wrote of the intentional reconciliation activities of three residential peace communities. The three chosen sprang from, but are not limited to, the three major strands of Christian denominations in Ireland: The Columbanus Community (Catholic), The Corrymeela Community (Presbyterian) and The Christian Renewal Centre (Church of Ireland). Because of the good reception of that book, I began to think about what might be the next step in my engagement with the subject. Upon reflection, it seemed like a natural development for me to focus on the two men whose lives together form the basis of this book.

Ken and Gerry, for their part, acknowledged that their story was important and that it needed to be told and preserved in order to encourage others to seek vocations for peace and reconciliation. In due course all agreed that I should write this book, and that they would help as best they could. Although I knew Northern Ireland quite well, having visited some twenty times, and having written three previous books on the province, it was still thought valuable that I was an 'outsider' with no 'axe to grind' in respect of either community. While it was vital that I be a knowledgeable writer, and myself a Christian, I was neither British nor Irish, neither Catholic nor Presbyterian. I am an American raised in the Anglican communion who teaches at a college founded by the Dutch Reformed Church.

Many people helped me along the way in Ireland. It has been an honour to work with the two principals. They are men of great integrity whom I respect very much indeed. They gave me a great deal of their time, and they opened doors to many other people. While both Gerry and Ken have read a draft of this book for accuracy, the views expressed here are mine, not theirs, and they should not be held responsible for what I have done with their testimony. Also, Val Newell and the good men at Clonard Monastery welcomed me to their tables for meals and into their hearts for encouragement. At Clonard I am particularly grateful for the confidence shown in me by Alec Reid. At Fitzroy Church, Sandra and James Rutherford helped in many crucial ways. Also in Belfast, Jim Lynn and Roddy Evans were of great help at a critical juncture.

In America I was helped by my home institution, Calvin College, with a travel grant from one of its research institutes. That allowed me to visit Northern Ireland repeatedly to interview participants and to do research in libraries. I thank James Bratt and Donna Romanowski of the Calvin Center for Christian Scholarship and Dean Janel Curry for her oversight of the grant. Finally, I thank my wife, Barbara, a busy academic author in her own right, who gave me encouragement and ideas throughout my work on this book. The few words of dedication on another page say too little about what her love and friendship means for my ongoing work on peace and reconciliation.

Ronald A. Wells
Advent, 2004

Why Are We Interested in the Friendship Between Ken Newell and Gerry Reynolds? What's at Stake?

Many good books have been written about 'the Troubles', the long-standing conflict between the two communities in Northern Ireland, the Protestant/Unionist and the Catholic/ Nationalist. This is not another book about the Troubles, though it is located in the context of the last thirty years of the conflicted history of the land in which the two communities cannot agree on a name (Northern Ireland, Ulster, The Six Counties, The North of Ireland). Rather, this is a book about a friendship forged within the Troubles. In a way, it can be seen as an anti-dote to them. This study of the friendship between Fr Gerry Reynolds and Rev Ken Newell will show three things: that people can transcend their communities of origin; that narratives of justice and forgiveness can have positive social outcomes; that telling this story offers a kind of icon of grace for the whole church.

These are Christian men. Their faith, forged in two different communities, would bring them together. The major result of their joint efforts – the Clonard-Fitzroy Fellowship – was honored in 1999 by being given the annual international peace prize from Pax Christi. If we would listen to their story, and the impacts they have had, it will be a graceful story that will show us all a way forward to a society of toleration, justice, pluralism and peace. But first, a few words of context are necessary.

There are many recent books on contemporary Northern Irish affairs that could offer us some context, but three stand out. We will refer to them in order to illumine the two worlds from which Ulster Catholics and Protestants come, thus showing how far the congregations at Fitzroy and Clonard had to move for their Fellowship to be created and to succeed. For the next few pages we will follow the contributions of four writers: Marianne Elliott, Professor of Irish History at Liverpool University; David McKittrick, for many years the award-winning correspondent in Northern Ireland for the London newspaper, *The Independent;* and Cecelia Clegg and Joseph Liechty whose thorough and path-breaking work on sectarianism is vital to understand.

Marianne Elliott's book, *The Catholics of Ulster* (2002), is an excellent guide on the subject. She was also a member of the Opsahl Commission (1992–93) which was the closest thing Northern Ireland has had to a South African-style 'truth and reconciliation commission'. It functioned somewhat like one, in receiving submissions about the Troubles from citizens and groups alike, and in making recommendations to the British and Irish governments. What comes through strongly in the Opsahl Commission, and in Elliott's discussion of it, is the way in which ordinary citizens articulated the several senses in which the Troubles were, and are, about religion and ethnic identity. While acknowledging the complicated 'shades of grey' that defy black-and-white analyses of religion's role in the conflict, Elliott agrees with the growing (but still minority chorus) that thinks the Troubles are about religion (for example, in the writing of Steve Bruce, Duncan Morrow, Brian Lambkin, Scott Appleby, Ronald Wells). But – and this is vital – the two communities see the mix of religion and politics in different ways. Protestants tend to enter the discussion from the religious end, and then later turn to politics. Catholics tend to enter the discussion from the political end, and then as the discussion develops, turn to religion. The Opsahl hearings echoed again and again with the Protestant assertion about the importance of religion in cultural identity, and with Catholic assertion about the central place of history and language in identity. As Elliott sums up in her fine set of essays, *The Long Road to Peace in Northern Ireland,* (2001): 'The bogeyman for Catholics was the state and its representatives; for Protestants it was the Catholic Church itself.'

The fear of Catholicism, and the distrust that follows, is deeply felt and agreed upon among a diversity of Protestants who might not agree on much else. Rev Robert Dickinson, a Moderator of the Presbyterian Church of Ireland in 1985, and noted conservative, who will appear again later in this book, wrote to the Opsahl Commission that Protestants

> see the political situation in clearly religious perspectives. ... They see the attempt to bring about a 'united Ireland' not only as an attack upon their political and constitutional well-being, but also as an attack upon their religious heritage, and an attempt to establish in Northern Ireland the dominance of the Roman Catholic Church. ... They see every aspect of the political, cultural, educational, medical, industrial, social and religious life of the Republic dominated, and often con-trolled, by the power and influence of the Roman Catholic Church.

Such statements begin to suggest why such a sizeable portion of the Protestant adult male population – thought to be about one third – are members of the Orange Order. That membership requires adherents 'to strenuously oppose the fatal errors and doctrines of the church of Rome'. Protestant opposition to Catholicism is also buttressed by perceptions that since the Troubles began most developments have gone in favour of the Nationalist, Catholic population. Even at that, some Protestants note ruefully that Catholics still complain about the slow 'progress' being made.

Protestant attitudes like these leave many Catholic and Nationalist people bewildered and angry. They believe that in-deed *they* have been the historic victims. They find it difficult to believe that Protestant fears about Catholic domination are sin-cere, but see them as only a cover up for simple bigotry. Also, they think that Protestant talk of loyalty to Britain is another way of re-asserting its ascendant position over the Catholic, Nationalist population. Catholics, for their part, freely admit that their religion is important to them and that, for example, they want a Christian education for their children conducted under the supervision of their own church, not the state, which they do not trust. But, they insist, their religious values do not dictate their attitudes towards Protestants and to the state.

Rather, their attitudes are guided by a belief in the justice of a united Ireland in which the political and human rights of all would be safeguarded.

In the time since the ceasefires in the early 1990s and the Agreement in 1998, the emphasis among religious peace-builders has been on reconciliation, even forgiveness, in political and cultural life. But for many Protestants (some would say most), there is little willingness to repent of past actions, and even less to ask the forgiveness of the Catholic, Nationalist community. Indeed many, though perhaps not most in this case, still tar the Catholic community with the same repugnant brush used on the IRA for its campaign of violence that cost so much human pain in the Protestant, Unionist community.

This is not the place to try to assess with finality on which side to place more of the blame for the culture of violence created by the Troubles. But even the most non-partisan and even-handed person – as the present writer would like to be – who looks forward to a culture of toleration and peace must say something about the nature of the society that caused the Troubles and what needs to be done if a way forward is to be found. David McKittrick's even-handed analysis of the contested state in Northern Ireland in the twentieth century (*Making Sense of the Troubles*, 2002), nevertheless makes a more persuasive explanatory case for the Nationalist, Catholic position about discrimination and intimidation than for the Unionist, Protestant belief in 'the will of the majority' that gave them the right to a half-century of 'ascendancy' in all areas of Northern Irish life. As McKittrick notes, the Protestant leadership in Northern Ireland used their majority vote to systematically deprive the Catholic community of political and human rights. The various governments in London were also aware of the unfair principles institutionalised by the local Ulster governments at Stormont. But the British parties – Conservative and Labour alike – did nothing to right the situation because they considered a loyal Northern Ireland to be an important part of national defence. Therefore, leadership from London was not forthcoming, and the

Unionists were allowed their undemocratic society within the United Kingdom.

In this regard, a judicious and careful assessment has been offered by Maurice Irvine in his book, *Faith and Faction* (1991). In a dozen economical but sensitively-written pages, he constructs a rather even balance sheet of remembered rights and wrongs perpetrated in the name of religion. But even the careful Irvine must come down somewhere, and the following riveting paragraph deserves quoting:

> While there are numerous obstacles to the dissolution of this communal division and to the growth of a normal integrated society in Northern Ireland, it is evident that the decisive one, that to which all others are subordinate, is the deep-seated hostility permeating the Protestant community to the Roman Catholic ethos. While it is not contested that there are some reasonable grounds for disquiet, it is argued that the virulence and intensity of the sentiment in the Ulster psyche is far beyond anything that can be justified by events in the past or by the present sociological realities. This neurotic fear can probably not be eradicated or moderated by anything the Irish Catholic community can do; its irrationality renders it impervious to outside influence. Its removal, if this is ever to come about, must derive from within the Protestant community itself.

One is afraid that evangelical Protestant readers of the above will say that academic liberals, attuned to the ecumenical movement, are ganging up on them again, and their defensiveness and resistance will once again stiffen. One can only say that we all need to hear another reading of the gospel: precisely because religion was so important in causing conflict, a re-configured religion is also vital in finding the way to peace. As we look to the Bible for guidance, we see that early in the story God seems to bestow his favour exclusively on a particular people. As the story unfolds, and especially after the resurrection of Jesus, the good news from God is meant for all. Finally, in the last part of the Bible, the universality of God's grace is revealed. Those who name the Name, who will sing the praises of the Almighty in endless songs, will come from all tribes, tongues and peoples. There will be, of course, the final boundary marking the faithful from the faithless – heaven and hell will exist – but the inhabitants of the two will not be chosen according to the human contingencies of politics, nationality, race, class and gender.

All Christian share a common prayer, the Lord's Prayer. The Reformation did not change that. About the plea to God that all Christians say ('thy kingdom come'), we do well to consult the Bible about what that kingdom will look like. We read that the kingdom will come in the morning, when time shall be no more, when all tears will be wiped from our eyes, when the lion and the lamb will lie down together – when, in short, there will be *shalom*. In that time and place, God, it seems, will not prefer a certain race (whites will not be over blacks) or gender (men will not be over women), or nationality (English will not be over Irish) or social class (the powerful will not be over the meek and lowly) or denomination (Presbyterians will not be over Catholics).

Because both readings of the Christian story are plausible, one can see the confusion possible: early in the story God's favour was exclusive, while in the post-resurrection era God's favour is inclusive – some would say universal. It is, one thinks, not that God changes his mind, but that the record we have of his revelation seems to develop over time. By the end of the Bible, it seems that God desires that all people come to him, to live in his favour and at peace with each other. This interpretation will cause its contemporary adherents to see their task of inclusion very differently from those who view their task as trying to maintain the boundaries between those chosen and those beyond the pale.

The pernicious virus of sectarianism, the social disease that Ken Newell, Gerry Reynolds and the Clonard-Fitzroy Fellowship sought to confront, was and is deeply imbedded in Northern Irish life. We should examine it briefly to name the ill that those in our story are determined to oppose. Sectarianism has been widely written about, but no book is as comprehensive as, or better suited to our purposes than, *Moving Beyond Sectarianism* (Dublin: Columba Press, 2001). The authors – Cecelia Clegg and Joseph Liechty – directed a five-year project of the same title, under the auspices of the Irish School of Ecumenics. The depth and breadth of their study is unlikely to be surpassed. Let us glean a few thoughts from their study that pertain to our subject.

The authors demonstrate, first, that sectarianism is more than just an attitude of the human heart. While it is surely that, it is much more than that. It has a systemic reality and it exists in communal forms (voluntary associations) and in institutional forms and structures (governmental, political and economic). Moreover, the mixing of religion and politics, while a legitimate exercise in a democracy, becomes sectarian when the religious loyalties of one group are invoked to the disadvantage of another group. Further, we all need boundary markers if our identities are to function in society: we need to come from somewhere, be connected to specific others and believe in something larger than our own personal preferences. However, it is when the legitimate needs for identity and belonging become distorted into devaluing, even demonising others, that it becomes sectarian. The authors carefully deconstruct the notion that people engaging in offensive sectarian activity really didn't mean anything bad by it, but they were only being true to themselves and to their own traditions. An example often given is the annual marching of the Protestant Orange Order which, the Order says, merely affirms a Loyalist identity in commemorating the past. That may well be true on one level. But, on a deeper level, Protestant marching cannot be isolated from a long heritage of intended intimidation and humiliation of the Catholic, Nationalist community. Peacebuilders, and those of us who would tell their story, owe a great debt to Clegg and Liechty for their excellent work. The fact that the Clonard-Fitzroy Fellowship received the Pax Christi award just prior to the appearance of the book suggests the convergence of ideas about how the way forward is to be understood.

The story of Gerry Reynolds and Ken Newell and their congregations is important as an example of how ordinary people in real time began to move beyond sectarianism, motivated by a new vision for a better future for all people in Ireland. It is also important to remember this in the context of the wider arena of peace-building. Following Paul Arthur, a leading political scientist in Ireland, we note that peace processes are begun by political leaders; so one gives full credit in Northern Ireland to John Hume, David Trimble and Gerry Adams, and on the international level to Bertie Ahern, Tony Blair and Bill Clinton . But, as Arthur insists, a peace process in itself is not reconciliation. It can only barely begin a journey back from the maelstrom of social disorder, bitterness and conflict, and forward towards peace, reconciliation and tolerance. In that journey the intermediate institutions of civil society will be vital if the peace process is to be successful.

In the case of Northern Ireland, the churches have long been dominant in society, and bear some responsibility for sowing the seeds of enmity and exclusion that grew into the Troubles. But, precisely because the churches were a large part of the cause of conflict they can also be transformed to be a major part of the cure. They must be open to a deeper living of the gospel – a gospel that supplants exclusion with inclusion, hatred with love, and zeal to confront and proselytise with a vision of tolerance in which each community's virtues are celebrated as a contribution to all. There must be a determination to move from 'there' to 'here' on the road to 'somewhere' called peace and reconciliation. Vital in the process will be the ability to tell each other the stories of each community – its joys and sorrow, its triumphs and tragedies, as well as the way some people have overcome and moved on. Such persons and groups will become 'icons of grace', as their stories are heard and as they motivate others. These stories of grace will accumulate, it is hoped, and then they can re-shape personal and collective memories.

Take, for example, the powerful story related by Seamus Heaney in his speech accepting the Nobel Prize in 1995. He recounts what is known as the Kingsmills massacre of January 1976, when ten Protestant workmen and their Catholic driver were held at gunpoint on a lonely stretch of road on their way home. One of the masked executioners demanded that if there were any Catholics among them they were to step out of the lineup. The assumption was that it was a loyalist, Protestant gang. Heaney writes:

> It was a terrible moment for him, caught between dread and witness, but he did make a motion to step forward. Then, the story goes, in that split second of decision, and in the relative cover of the winter evening darkness, he felt the hand of the Protestant worker next to him take his hand for a second that said no, don't move, we'll not betray you, nobody needs to know what faith or party you belong to. All in vain, however, for the man stepped out of line; but instead of finding a gun to his temple, he was pushed away as the gunmen opened fire on those remaining in the line, for these were not Protestant terrorists, but members, presumably, of the Provisional IRA.

Heaney concludes: 'The birth of the future we desire is surely in the contraction which that terrified Catholic felt when another hand gripped his hand, not in the gunfire that followed so absolutely.'

The thesis argued here is this: that as people hear compelling stories of grace they too will find ways to attest in their lives the hope that 'deep in our hearts we do believe that we shall overcome someday'. They thereby can contribute to delegitimating the politics of force and the legitimating of democratic politics in a society moving towards peace and tolerance.

Under the leadership of Fitzroy Presbyterian's pastor, Rev Ken Newell, the congregation reached out to the Church of the Most Holy Redeemer, attached to Clonard Monastery. Through the close friendship between Newell and Fr Gerry Reynolds of Clonard, the two churches and their communities were able to speak with a prophetic voice to the Troubles, first mainly in religious terms, but then also having an important impact on political reconciliation.

With this context established, we now return specifically to Gerry Reynolds and Ken Newell. Our two comrades are ordained clergy, one a Catholic priest of the Redemptorist order, the other a minister in the Presbyterian Church in Ireland. Their shared identity as Christians has allowed them to transcend, not disown, the respective cultures from which they come. So, Ken has been profoundly shaped by a Northern Irish Protestant and Unionist culture, while Gerry has been molded by an Irish Catholic and Nationalist culture. In being friends, they are not giving up on those particular and peculiar aspects of their own cultural backgrounds. But Reynolds and Newell also see how much they – as Christians – have in common, and how naturally they have come to see, as their friendship has deepened, the worth of the other's cultural values.

Reynolds is a few years older than Newell. The priest was born prior to the Second World War, the minister just after it began. But they both grew up in the years immediately follow-ing the war, one in the Nationalist culture of Limerick in the Irish Republic, the other in a Loyalist section of the Protestant heartland in Belfast. Although Gerry agrees with the Catholic and southern Irish view of political life, he is aware that the peo-ple he serves, the Catholics of west Belfast, grew up with a dif-ferent understanding of what it means to be Catholic in their locale. Reynolds' people around the neighbourhood of Clonard Monastery feel a deep alienation from the social and political milieu of Northern Ireland. One observer has said that these sen-timents can be characterised as 'a culture of grievance'. Gerry has come to understand that culture, and since he is dedicated to the people there, he shares its feelings. He joins his people in feeling deeply the effects of years of discrimination, intimid-ation and political impotence.

A visitor to Clonard Monastery need only go a few short blocks from the door of the adjoining Church of the Most Holy Redeemer to see evidences of those feelings of alienation and of sorrowful memories. The reminders are dramatically present on Bombay Street, a small street located near the juncture of the Protestant Shankill Road neighbourhood and the Catholic Falls Road neighbourhood. The Catholic, Nationalist community in the Falls area around Clonard date the arrival of the Troubles in their area on 12 August 1969, when a loyalist group burned down a large number of dwellings on Bombay Street in an attempt, literally, to 'burn out' the Catholic residents of the neighbourhood. Today the homes are rebuilt and Bombay Street is a quiet and tidy road whose peacefulness belies the years of torment and anxiety that befell its residents. On one side of Bombay Street, just as it bends back toward the soaring height of the Monastery, one sees part of 'the peace line', a very tall and formidable wall built by the security forces to divide the warring communities, in order to keep some semblance of 'peace' between them. But, just at the bend of the road, and abutting the large wall, is a small enclosure that allows one to dignify remembrance. It is a small, almost shrine-like place. One pushes back the gate and sits on the bench provided for visitors, and notes the large plaque, made of what looks to be bronze, on which are named all the people of the neighbourhood who have died in direct relation to the Troubles – on one side the names of those 'on active service', and on the other the 'civilians'. At the top of the list of civilian dead is the name of a Redemptorist Brother, Michael Morgan, shot dead on 20 July 1922 by the British Army. It seems they were looking for snipers and one soldier saw Brother Michael at a window in Clonard, about a hundred metres away. The soldier shot first and asked questions later. The Bombay Street section of the Falls Road had its first victim of the Troubles – although two generations before their re-starting in 1969. Further down the road one sees a large mural painted on the windowless side of a home, on which is depicted the night of 12 August 1969, when the homes of Bombay Street were alight and people running from them. Emblazoned on that mural are enjoinders that viewers not forget the events of Bombay Street.

The short walk back to the monastery on a recent winter day can be made quickly, and for this writer, in silence. On entering the sanctuary of the Church of the Most Holy Redeemer one heard the recorded singing of the well-known song written by Jacques Berthier of the Taizé Community, 'Jesus, remember me, when you come into your kingdom.' I lit a candle in the names of my adult children back in America, and added the name of Michael Morgan to my prayers. Such are the lingering memories of west Belfast, and the lives of people ministered to by Gerry Reynolds from Clonard Monastery.

The world in which Ken Newell grew up, by contrast, was quite different. His family lived on the Shore Road, a mainly working-class and Loyalist area of North Belfast. It was here that he unconsciously imbibed typical Protestant ideas, values and practices. Through the influence of his father, Norman, whom he greatly admired, he was introduced to Orangeism, and at eighteen he joined the Loyal Orange Lodge 1322 which met about half a mile from his home, close to Dunmore Park.

He vividly recalls his father coming home in the evening from work in the Ulster Transport Authority, where he was an active trade union man, quickly eating his dinner and then re-porting for duty at York Street Police Station as a B-Special, a quasi-military police force seen by Catholics as part of the regime most oppressive to them. As a child and teenager Ken was unaware of the negative impact the B-Specials had in Catholic and Nationalist areas throughout Northern Ireland.

Among his peer group Ken listened to numerous stories of how Fenians and Catholics had done many nasty things to Protestants and so were not to be trusted. It was acceptable to work alongside Catholics at places of employment, but socialis-ing as friends or getting to know each other's faith or church was frowned upon. One learned about Catholics and their church from Protestants or ex-Catholics who had become Protestants, with the result that nothing positive was ever learned and noth-ing complimentary was ever communicated. No practising Catholic was ever invited to answer the allegations made or point out misunderstanding or blatant misrepresentation. In young Ken's world one was forbidden to go into a Catholic church or attend a Catholic service. It was said 'the Devil might get you and lead you astray!'

One Sunday afternoon, in his early teens, after attending

worship in his local Presbyterian church, he went for a walk up to Belfast Castle with some friends. As they were passing the Little Flower Oratory, a Catholic church on the Somerton Road, the group noticed some people going into the church. Without thinking, some of the teenagers lifted stones, threw them at the worshippers and then sprinted for the spacious grounds of the castle. As he was turning to run away he noticed the face of one of the worshippers who had turned and caught his eye. It was not a glance of anger but sorrow. He often wondered if the man had said a prayer for him. Forty years later, when he returned to the scene of this incident, it was to commend the Evangelical-Roman Catholic Theological Conferences to the local bishop.

When Ken turned eighteen he moved consciously from merely attending the local Seaview Presbyterian Church to committing his life to Christ. His mother Eva had a strong and practical faith. As he moved into his teenage years, the ministers of Seaview Presbyterian Church had a quiet but effective influence on his thinking and life-direction. His faith-attraction to Christ and to evangelical Christianity was slow and gradual, but started taking root in his spirit at this time. His understanding of the faith was enthusiastic, fundamentalist, and right-wing politically. But socially he had no Catholic friends and emotionally lived in a kind of spiritual apartheid. That was not necessarily of his choosing; it was the product of growing up in a divided city with a mind and spirit molded by the atmosphere of mistrust. He was not unusual but typical.

Halfway through his university course, Ken was urged to consider the ministry of the Presbyterian Church by the youth leaders in Seaview Presbyterian Church. They had been role-models in the development of his faith and their suggestions were therefore taken seriously by him. Slowly a sense of calling emerged and he applied to the Presbytery of North Belfast to be accepted as a candidate for the ministry.

When he entered Assembly's College in 1964 to train for the ministry of the Presbyterian Church, Ken was still right-wing, fundamentalist, suspicious of theological education, a chaplain

in LOL 1322, strongly anti-Catholic, and believed that the Pope
was the anti-Christ. In one or two marginal areas he was re-
thinking his faith, but those around him were not generally
aware of this. Further, Ken accepted the ideas of his own tradition that Catholic Nationalists were, at best, a nuisance to be tol-
erated in this corner of British Ireland and, at worst, a subversive
element to be distrusted and contained. At the base of that
Protestant culture was an anxiety and fear about being over-
whelmed by the numerically-superior Nationalists in an all-
Ireland context, and about the pernicious 'foreign' power of the
international Catholic Church.

I was eager to learn about the experiences Ken Newell would
have had to go through and the graces he would have to experience in order to be able to find a way to bridge the world of his
upbringing and that of the people of Clonard. That sort of journey of faith between religious worlds – from ghetto mainten-
ance to bridge-building – is captured by the respected Jesuit
scholar, Fr Michael Hurley, who told me that 'the churches were
once part of the problem; they are now part of the solution'.
Gerry Reynolds and Ken Newell take it as their calling to be part
of the solution. Their story is an encouragement to all who wish
to catch a glimpse of a kingdom vision, of a world headed toward reconciliation and peace.

CHAPTER TWO

Preparing the Way: Antecedent Attitudes and Events

The premise of telling the story of the friendship between Gerry Reynolds and Ken Newell is that they are two ordinary men; they worked among ordinary people, but together they were able to accomplish extraordinary things. The two friends would be the first to stress their unexceptional qualities, while at the same time giving thanks for what they were enabled to do, as they would say, by the grace of God. While interviewing them I always noted their wish to divert attention from themselves.

In fact, there was a great deal of important activity that laid the groundwork for their work and that preceded their friendship and the founding of the Clonard-Fitzroy Fellowship. Also, there were other parallel activities of many people, whose work either encouraged Ken and Gerry or helped to implement a shared vision of peace and reconciliation in Northern Ireland. Over the next few pages let us look into the wide range of ideas, feelings and actions that made way for, and bear upon, the friendship in which we are interested.

In 1972, Ken Newell went out to the island of Timor in Indonesia under the auspices of the Presbyterian Church to teach New Testament at the Theological Academy of Kupang in Timor. Along with his wife, Valerie, and young son, Tim, Ken anticipated a fairly long stay there. Just as he was about to leave Belfast in July 1972, the tragic events of Bloody Friday occurred. Ken vividly recalls sitting in his car in a traffic jam in central Belfast, 150 metres from the Oxford Street Bus Station, recoiling with fear in a way previously unknown to him. On that day the Irish Republican Army exploded the largest number of bombs on any given day of the entire span of the Troubles. In the midst of that strife and the anxiety it caused, Ken vowed that when or if he returned from Indonesia he would dedicate himself to join others in overcoming the anger and bitterness that had caused such violence.

Soon after settling in to their lives in Indonesia, Ken and Val had some experiences that would push them along a road that would lead back to reconciliation work in Belfast. On one level, Ken's work with Indonesian students gave him an insight that was to be long-lasting, that Christianity is a minority religion in Indonesia and the wider world, and that one should emphasise ideas and attitudes that would foster solidarity and unity among fellow Christians of all denominations. On another level, out there in Indonesia Ken and Val began to learn about Irish Catholics in ways that might not have happened back in Belfast. It seems that there were few native English-speakers at all in their part of Timor, so sometimes Australian and American missionaries would get together just to speak English and have some fellowship. Ken later recalled how he made his first true friend among Irish Catholics.

> One day, after we were there about six months, our front door was knocked, and when we opened it, a chap with a broad Irish accent said, 'Hello, I'm Noel Carroll from Dundalk. I believe your wife was born there too.' He had heard there were three Ulster Protestants on the island and he wanted to come to wish us well. Noel was a priest in the Society of the Divine Word. About once every three months he would come from the mountains where his parish was to pay us a visit. He was the first 'real' friend of ours who was Catholic.
>
> Noel was a very keen student of the Bible, and since I was teaching New Testament at the Theological Academy, we used to get into some great discussions, which lasted for hours. We mostly discussed the reasons why I thought the Protestant faith was right and why Noel thought the Catholic faith was right. Our exchanges were friendly as well as honest, though we concentrated mostly on the things we disagreed about.
>
> After several discussions, we began to talk about Jesus Christ and our relationship to him, and what he meant in our

lives. Slowly I began to see the basic thing we had in common was our love for and dedication to Jesus Christ. I began to discover that in Christ we were not opponents, enemies, opposites, but rather brothers of the same master, children of the same heavenly father. In that discovery, for both Noel and myself, thirty years of conditioning to suspicion, distrust, keeping-your-distance, were removed. Old wounds of hostility were healed and inherited false images of each other's churches were removed. We still had our disagreements on certain ideas, but the basis of our friendship was Jesus.

The family was not to stay in Indonesia as long as Ken and Val had anticipated. In 1975, they returned to Belfast for the birth of their second child, Jennie. Some family medical issues arose, and this resulted in advice from the Overseas Board of the Presbyterian Church not to return to Indonesia. To the great delight and surprise of Ken and Val, there was a vacancy at the Fitzroy Presbyterian Church on University Street. And so Ken Newell, now only in his early thirties, was installed as the pastor of Fitzroy on 15 January 1976.

While no one could have predicted where Fitzroy Church would go in the next quarter century, now looking back, the journey has been little short of astonishing. In 1976 Fitzroy would have positioned itself within the evangelical wing of the Presbyterian Church, but was in no way extreme or fundamentalist. But like almost all churches in Northern Ireland, it was not immune from the subtle influences of sectarianism which touched everything and everyone. There were some examples of 'hard-line attitudes', but they were never dominant. As to political viewpoints, Fitzroy Church would have been comfortable within the moderate brand of Unionism. Also, as the Alliance Party emerged, there would have been some support for it. There would have been next to no Nationalists nor supporters of Ian Paisely's brand of Unionism. But, the transformation of the congregation over the next quarter century was such that, in 1999, it was given the prestigious award by Pax Christi for its reconciliation work with Clonard monastery. Well might one wonder how Fitzroy developed its spiritual orientation beyond traditional Ulster evangelical attitudes into becoming, in a deeply divided city, a beacon of hope in promoting positive inter-church ecumenical initiatives and influential reconciliation activities. While Ken Newell is not the whole story of Fitzroy's transformation, everyone associated with Fitzroy and Clonard insist that in the absence of Ken's leadership and determination the journey would not have been taken. Part of the genius of his leadership was to empower many others to move in directions that, without his encouragement, they would not have gone.

We have a chance to catch a substantial glimpse of the tendency of Ken's early thinking, and the way in which his leadership would unfold at Fitzroy Church. In the spring of 1977 a study group was established by the Inter-Church Relations Board of the Presbyterian Church in Ireland (PCI). Its task was to study, and to comment on, the document *Confessing Christ Today*, which had been published by the World Council of Churches at its meeting in Nairobi in 1975. All the constituent member churches of the WCC were to make their submissions. The PCI committee asked Ken Newell to write a discussion paper to get a conversation underway in Ireland about this important document. Ken's task was to summarise the main points of it and to pose questions, especially as they had bearing on the meaning of *Confessing Christ Today* in the context of Northern Ireland. We can glean some key points from Ken's discussion paper that will enable us to see the ways that Ken was urging the PCI to develop, and his early goals for Fitzroy Church.

First, Ken articulated an important theme on Reformed theology, that confessing Jesus to be Lord is a thorough-going confession. It is not confined to the inner spiritual life of the Christian, but must encompass the whole range of human relationships and institutions, i.e., social, economic and political. Moreover, Newell suggested that the reconciling power of the gospel in individual terms will be blocked if the church is not utilising that power in societal terms as well. Ken challenged his denomination with the idea that we cannot be right with God if we are wrong with our neighbours. Therefore, in view of the bitter division between the churches in Northern Irish society, it was not clear that the churches could have much in the way of effective witness at all.

Second, *Confessing Christ Today* pointed to the social and religious structures that obscure the gospel's power: most importantly race, class and gender. Ken asked clearly how much the PCI's identification with the politics of Protestant privilege would tend to obscure the church's gospel witness. He then specified the differences between Presbyterian and Catholic responses to recent events, i.e., that the former mostly spoke from a Unionist position and the latter from a Nationalist one; Ken observed that the churches seem to speak *from*, not *to*, the Troubles.

Third, Newell stressed that the church's confession should be unequivocal in its commitment to evangelism. In this connection, he stressed the word 'whole': that evangelism was to be a whole gospel, preached through the whole world, and – vitally – by the whole church. Ken thought the last point was crucial, because 'disunity in mission and evangelism not only undermines the credibility of our reconciling gospel but causes unnecessary competition, considerable overlapping of work and increasingly poor relationships between the churches'. Such a commitment on the part of the Presbyterian Church in Ireland would necessarily mean repentance from the association with political and economic privilege and from reluctance to work closely with all other Christian denominations.

Early in his ministry, then, Ken was already well on the road to being a pastoral leader who would call his people to a thorough evangelism, in which the proclamation of the gospel would be as much social as personal, and as much interdenominationally Christian as peculiarly Presbyterian. And, in view of the contested context in Northern Ireland, one of the keys matters for his church leadership would be reconciliation between Presbyterians and Roman Catholics. But, as any good leader knows, Ken understood that one couldn't get too far out in front of the people. Ken did not have a pre-packaged masterplan of the path down which he wanted to guide Fitzroy; rather he depended on the Holy Spirit to show him the way forward for the congregation, as he said, 'inch by inch'. He was also aware that people change slowly and need to be given time and good biblical reasons for the direction being taken.

By the late 1970s the scene was set for the first tentative steps on the road to reconciliation. Ken felt very strongly that he and the Fitzroy people should reach out to the people of the nearby Catholic parish, St Malachy's Church. One day in the autumn of 1978 he walked the 100 metres down Magdala Street to the house of Fr Denis Newberry, the local Catholic curate. He was given a very courteous welcome. As they talked in the weeks and months that followed, it was suggested that the two churches begin doing things together in friendship, and the two congregations began to undertake some joint initiatives. They included services marking the annual Week of Prayer for Christian Unity and the first ever Joint Christmas Carol Service held in Fitzroy in 1978 led by clergy from St Malachy's, All Saints Parish Church (Anglican Church of Ireland) in University Street and Rugby Avenue Congregational Churches. Fitzroy was packed in an unforgettable Christmas celebration in a city known at the time as the Murder Capital of Europe. When Fr Denis was transferred to Co Down, the leadership in St Malachy's became occupied on other fronts, so there was little scope for the relationship with Fitzroy. As a result, the cooperation faded for several years. Later it was to be reawakened under Fr Anthony Curran.

In retrospect, these activities would appear relatively non-threatening. At Fitzroy, those who felt uncomfortable were a small but significant and respected group both within and outside the Kirk Session. Because the congregation was having an internal debate on the issues of reconciliation and peacemaking in Belfast, there was evident appreciation of steps being taken as well division, uncertainty, and resistance. Most members expressed their views to each other in mature and considered ways, but some words spoken in anger revealed underlying attitudes that were decidedly anti-Catholic and sectarian. In this atmosphere, which persisted for about three years, Ken kept his composure and returned again and again to the gospel, with its unavoidable challenge to love our enemies and to bridge to those from whom we are distant with the kindness of Christ in our hearts. This message, he thought, had to be lived out on the streets of Belfast or it was not worth living out anywhere in the world.

Eventually less than ten families out of the 500 associated with Fitzroy decided to leave. It was a sad occasion for those who left and for those who stayed, but the majority of the people remained faithful to the congregation. The loss was more than compensated by the fact that many new and younger families were being attracted to Fitzroy. Many of them were motivated by a desire to be part of a church that lived out its faith in meaningful and relevant ways in Belfast. They were aware that if political reconciliation was ever to be achieved (and there was no sign of it on the horizon at that time) then Christians in the churches should be giving a lead and demonstrating in practical ways that it is possible to build new and inclusive relationships. Over these three tense years, many new families joined the congregation. Several of these new members to whom I spoke told me that they joined Fitzroy because of Ken's (and the elders') policy of spiritual, ecclesiastical and political openness, not in spite of it.

Ken was also reaching out in political terms. He attended three of the major Peace Marches through Belfast with several members of Fitzroy. These marches were led by ordinary people, students from Queen's and some ecumenical clergy. But Ken was surprised to see so few of his fellow-Presbyterian ministers present. There were some Presbyterian ministers prominent in the crowds of marchers, but most of them had been, like Ken, missionaries of the Presbyterian Church who had lived overseas and had now returned. He wondered to himself that if Jesus taught that God's blessing rested on those who worked for peace and he calls them his children, then why more ministers aren't giving a lead to their members in the ministry of peace-

making. Many questions cropped up in Ken's mind: Why were
they sitting comfortably at home? Were they afraid? Did they
have no spiritual passion for this work of grace? Were they
keeping their heads down to protect their positions rather than
giving a courageous lead towards a better future shaped by the
values and vision of the gospel? Do those who leave the country
and live abroad see the malaise at the heart of the community
more clearly than those who stay at home? Is the gospel about
going to heaven when you die rather than living out Christ's life
and love on the conflict-ridden and blood-stained streets of
Belfast in the here and now? Thinking back to his own comments in *Confessing Christ Today*, Ken sometimes wondered if
there was a future for his way of thinking in the Presbyterian
Church in Ireland.

In short, during those early years of Ken's ministry back in
Belfast, he was experiencing both criticisms in his own congregation and a kind of alienation from what seemed to be the
dominant Presbyterian mind-set of non-engagement with
peacemaking and reconciliation activities. Once in a while he
even wondered about his own vocation to the ministry because
the future of the country sometimes did not look bright. It was at
this low point for Ken – spiritually and humanly – that the
Charismatic Renewal swept through Ireland. While Ken was
never really carried away with charismatic enthusiasm, he
would readily admit today that the vitality of the Renewal, and
the dynamic of the new friendships made through it, were the
refreshments he needed at the time. It was also what Fitzroy
needed too, at least in the estimation of Philip Mateer, then a recent graduate of Queen's, who was elected an elder in 1978. For
Mateer, the Renewal brought a sense of release from older, sup-
posedly tried-and-true ways of the Presbyterian Church, both in
terms of worship style and of the relationship with the Roman
Catholic community. He later recalled his early years as an elder
– in the flush of enthusiasm brought by Renewal – as a time of
hope and expectation when all political and secular indexes in
Northern Ireland were quite bleak.

During Ken's initial acquaintance with the Charismatic Renewal he was reading Calvin's *Institutes* on a regular and systematic basis. He later recalled that this theological rigour was a sound counter-balance to the possible emotional excesses of the Renewal. He was also guided by the example of David Watson, Canon of York Minster in England, who always wanted the Renewal to avoid individual excesses and to keep renewed spiritedness in service to the whole church. Ken also credits the friendships he made among renewal clergy – both Protestant and Catholic – with his being able to find himself again after the discouragements of his early years in the ministry. Primary among the new friends who brought Ken to a new place, personally and professionally, was Rev Cecil Kerr, the best known Irish person in the Renewal. Kerr had been Church of Ireland chaplain at Queen's during Ken's student years. Kerr later went on to have an internationally-acclaimed ministry among both Protestants and Catholics, in both the North and the South of Ireland. For many years he was the director of the Christian Renewal Centre in Rostrevor, near the border between Northern Ireland and the Republic of Ireland. While Kerr is rightly acclaimed for his public career, a ministry for which he is not well known was that of encouragement to clergy who felt a call to the work of reconciliation, but who were struggling against resistance in their local churches. Ken recalls several points in his life and ministry when the quiet counsel of Cecil Kerr was vital to his carrying on. In 1982 Kerr and Newell organised a service of praise and all-night prayer vigil at Fitzroy Church. Invitations went out from Rostrevor, and representatives from all Christian denominations came to the church on University Street that night. Ken was in charge of the liturgy, and some Fitzroy folk told me of their belief that what he wrote reads as well now as it did when spoken then:

> We are people made one by the love of Christ our Saviour and Lord. We have been changed as people by the grace of our Lord Jesus Christ. Gone is the pride that desires to dominate; gone is the anger that wants to undermine. By his Holy

Spirit we want to listen to each other's hurts and fears and build together a community fit for us all to live in, furnished with the generosity, justice and compassion of Jesus Christ.

Ken Newell was given a new sense of confidence and purpose by the Renewal movement and especially through the encouragement and support of Cecil Kerr.

Almost twenty years later, Ken was asked to join others in Rostrevor in honouring Cecil Kerr's twenty-five years of ministry at the Christian Renewal Centre. Ken wrote the following moving tribute to Kerr:

> At a time when I felt I couldn't stay and work in the claustrophobic atmosphere of Northern Ireland, you and the Centre provided me with the space to breathe.
>
> In a profoundly divided community. you and the Centre showed me that the gospel really unites, and that our unity is even deeper than our divisions.
>
> From a background steeped in the rationalism of Presbyterianism you and the Centre helped me to explore the heart as well as honour the mind.
>
> In a culture that pressures us into keeping our heads down and mouths shut, you and the Centre encouraged me to see that the opposite of faith is not unbelief but inactivity.
>
> In a life conducive to overwork and inner weariness, you and the Centre provided me with an oasis of peace, rest and refreshment.
>
> In a calling to work for reconciliation despite it being the concern of a small minority, you and the Centre offered me a place where I could be affirmed, encouraged and reminded that I was not alone and that many others are walking the same path.

Unknown to Ken – but of great relevance for his future friendship with the people at Clonard Monastery, the Charismatic Renewal would have another impact. Fr Christopher McCarthy (known affectionately by all as Fr Christy) was a Catholic priest of the Redemptorist order who was to complete his career at Clonard after a varied ministry that included parish missions and university teaching on several continents. Fr Christy was encouraged to return to Belfast, where he had ministered earlier in his career, by the rector of the Redemptorist house in Limerick, Fr Gerry Reynolds, who himself would later replace Christy after his death and who would have such an impact on Ken Newell and Fitzroy Church. Fr Christy was by nature a vivacious person whose infectious love for life would have great impact on all who knew him. His main calling at Clonard in the time of his service there (1976 to his death in 1983) was to empower the people of the Church of the Most Holy Redeemer in the search for peace and reconciliation with Protestants. Christy saw that the openness to the leading of the Holy Spirit in the Renewal could be just the avenue God had provided to allow the people to reach out in new ways and to be reached by others. Yet, he was in the last stages of a painful, crippling illness that would soon confine him to a chair, so he was a bit reluctant to begin this new venture. But, unexpected events would soon overtake Christy's reluctance in an extraordinary way.

Two Lynn brothers – Paddy and Jim – were born and grew up in the greater Clonard area of west Belfast, and were faithful Catholics who were much in evidence in the life of the Church of the Most Holy Redeemer. Both had been hitherto unknown to public events, but certain incidents in their lives would have important consequences for them and others. Jim worked for many years in the engineering department of an employer in Belfast. He was the only Catholic in the area where he worked. While some of his Protestant co-workers were decent enough to him, a few of them were openly hostile, doing everything possible to make Jim's work life unbearable. Some of them would use their superior knowledge of the Bible to embarrass Jim and make him feel uncomfortable about his religion. From these experiences, Jim realised there was a need for a Bible study to educate Catholic men and women so they would be able to answer criticisms of their faith and beliefs, so he asked Fr Christy to start one.

At little bit later, in the mid-1970s, more dramatic incidents among the Lynn brothers would push things further. A brother of Paddy and Jim had been shot and severely injured. That, as well as the general chaos and violence of the Troubles, had greatly burdened Paddy. On one day when Paddy was particularly despondent, he was making his way home, feeling rather hopeless. His friend, Dr Roddy Evans, was later to write about what happened:

> He decided to sit down on a street wall for a rest. All of a sudden, the army and an IRA unit opened fire on each other. A woman opened her street door to urge Paddy to seek shelter in the safety of her home. But Paddy continued to sit there in his misery. Later as he made for home, he passed the open door of Saint Oliver Plunkett's Church, so he decided to go in for another rest. As he sat in the silence of the church, he felt a presence envelope him and heard a voice distinctly saying 'Paddy, I have work for you.' Paddy walked out into the night a different man.

Describing his experiences later, Paddy said, 'It was like walking on a beach beside the sea on a sunny day. Then a soft summer breeze touched me and passed on.' Some weeks later, Paddy attended a function held in the church hall attached to Clonard monastery. Pushing his way through the crowd, Father McCarthy sought out Paddy, completely unaware of what had happened to him. As he greeted Paddy, Fr Christy asked, 'What should we do in this present situation in Belfast?' Paddy replied, 'You should begin a Bible study group.' Fr Christy immediately answered, 'We will have our first one next Thursday evening here at Clonard.'

While some might possibly question the authenticity of Paddy Lynn's experience of the Holy Spirit, we can report that all around him believed it to be true and acted upon that belief. Fr Christy, it should be added, went a step further with Paddy's experience. He asked Paddy to tell his entire story to a Cistercian monk and priest who was visiting Clonard. Fr Aidan Cusack heard Paddy's testimony and later he assured Christy of his own conviction that Paddy had indeed had an authentic visitation of the Holy Spirit. With this sort of encouragement and intervention, Christy went ahead with his Bible studies among the people of Clonard. But he was looking for ways to include Protestants. As fellow Clonard priest Fr Alec Reid was later to say of Christy, he developed a strong vocation to reach out to the Protestant community 'to remove the myths and misunderstandings from the minds of some of those from that community'.

Christy was invited to a home on the Malone Road with a mixed Protestant-Catholic group, some of whom were associated with Moral Re-Armament. It was the home of Winifred Hind, who with her husband, Bishop John Hind, had served many years in China at the Trinity College Fukien Mission. That evening Christy met a person whose words and actions gave him the opening for which he was hoping. She was Ellie McDermot, by then a quite elderly lady. Her father had been mayor of Derry during the 1940s and he had participated in some of the worst workings of Unionist gerrymandering that had willfully deprived the majority Catholic population of its political and human rights. During the course of the evening Mrs McDermot apologised to Christy for the wrongs her family had perpetrated on his people. He later recalled that 'the sincerity of the apology from that old lady struck me like a blow in the chest. It was the first time I had heard some one from her class admit to the wrongs that had been done by her people.'

After that, Christy knew what he wanted to do, and he invited some of the Protestants he had met at the Hind home to come to join his Thursday night Bible class. Among those invited were Dr George and Mrs Ruth Dallas, of whom more below, when we will discuss the transition from religious to political reconciliation. George Dallas later said how important it was for Protestants to make the journey up to Clonard, to study the Bible with Catholics in their own neighbourhood. 'For some of us it helped greatly to meet in a Bible Study Group with Catholics from 'the grassroots'. All were people who have suffered from discrimination and harassment caused by the unjust society we have created. And instead of being bitter as we expect (and almost demand), we found in them qualities of generosity, graciousness and forgiveness which we knew, in spite of all our supposed advantages as Protestants, we did not have.' A conversation between George Dallas and Jim Lynn was to stay with George for the rest of his life. As he later told Roddy Evans:

> For me the most devastating experience was when one of our new friends told me how his life was made a hell every day at work by a bully-boy who also intimidates other Protestant workers. Ironically our friend was not seeking sympathy or even understanding but was deploring his own lack of forgiveness for his persecutor. A dozen such bully-boys can terrorise a large factory, and make it impossible for Catholics to work there. I realised as never before the injustice of our dominance which at all levels depends ultimately on the threat of sectarian murder. About the same time, having begun to understand more about what we needed to repent of, and a little about repentance itself, I began to think of what repentance must mean for our community in relation to Ireland. Surely it must mean a humble and glad acceptance of ourselves fully as Irish people, as we were always meant to be, not Irish and British as well, or any other formula that allows us to go on feeling superior. Unless our community finds this kind of repentance and learns to care for all the people of Ireland, there will always be violence in this country.

The evening at the Malone Road house had been organised by people associated with Moral Re-Armament, which organisation would come to represent another element of Fr Christy's wide-ranging interests and influences. That movement had been founded by an American, Dr Frank Buchman, and it had a considerable following among thoughtful people interested in peace, especially during the years immediately follow the Second World War. Much of the Catholic hierarchy was either uninterested or opposed to Moral Re-Armament because of its Protestant origins. But Fr Christy was interested, both because of its ideas about peace and reconciliation and because of the genuine friendship shown by the visionary people associated with it.

In London the rector of All Saints Church, Dulwich, was leading a discussion group in 1979-80 with members of his congregation. One person asked that the situation in Northern

Ireland be added to their topics. It was through the initiative of some Moral Re-Armament people present that the contact was made with colleagues in Belfast, and then with Fr Christy at Clonard, with the idea of bringing a group from Clonard over to London. A strong link between All Saints, Dulwich and The Church of the Most Holy Redeemer, Clonard was established and many profitable and friendly visits between the two went on in the ensuing years. Jim Lynn was especially important in maintaining that connection. Another spin-off from that connection is also important. In 1979, to coincide with the Pope's visit to Ireland, the prominently-placed Anglican clergyman, John Austin Baker, preached a powerful and much commented-upon sermon. Baker was, at the time, Canon of Westminster Abbey and Chaplain to the Speaker of the House of Commons. He expressed his sense of shame at what England had done to Ireland over the years. Christy heard about the sermon from some Irish Protestant friends and, on the strength of it, he invited Baker to preach at Clonard in January 1982, during the Week of Prayer for Christian Unity. Baker's presentations at Clonard were regarded as stunningly appealing by those who heard them. Baker, it might be added, was later appointed Bishop of Salisbury; and he was invited again to Ireland via McCarthy, this time to St Patrick's Cathedral, Armagh, where he was the first ever Anglican bishop to preach there.

Fr Christy was much encouraged with these various successes in Protestant-Catholic interactions in and around Clonard monastery. By then, around 1980, he was always looking for new ways to expand those kinds of relationships. Another unexpected entry into Christy's life from a Presbyterian source – this time Ken Newell – came in early 1981.

We should recall that this was a particularly low point in the history of the Troubles. Early in the premiership of Margaret Thatcher there were several signal events that would put Northern Irish affairs on a downward spiral that would take many years to reverse. The demand by the Republican prisoners in the Maze prison (known by its former name, Long Kesh, to the Nationalist Catholic community) that they be treated as political prisoners was rejected by Mrs Thatcher, who advocated treating them like non-political criminals. This dispute escalated into a hunger strike which brought a deep sense of polarisation in Northern Irish life. In the end, ten Republican prisoners starved themselves to death. The most notable was Bobby Sands, who died in May 1981, after sixty-six days on strike. Sands' memory moved deeply and quickly into the lore of Republicanism, and the ranks of the Irish Republican Army grew markedly. Mrs Thatcher's determination to allow the prisoners to die, along with her triple rejection of the recommendations by the think tank, 'The New Ireland Forum,' moved the IRA to the spectacular bombing of the Conservative Party convention hotel in Brighton, England, a blast that missed the Prime Minister but killed five others. The early 1980s, then, was a particularly difficult time.

In April of that hard year of 1981, the BBC in Northern Ireland, Radio Ulster, asked Ken Newell to take 'Thought for the Day,' a short programme of religious reflection. Ken did so, and spoke for several days on the Beatitudes. In his last programme – broadcast when Bobby Sands was well into his fatal hunger strike – Ken spoke on the passage from Matthew's gospel, 'Blessed are the peacemakers for God shall call them his children.' He noted that Robert Kee's excellent series on Irish history was just then running on BBC television, and that the secular viewpoint drawn from that series would offer little hope that the Irish people, especially the Northern Irish, would be able to escape the vicious and violent cycle of history. Ken also spoke of recently having attended a charismatic, ecumenical meeting in Belfast, at which several tapestries were displayed. One was quite moving to him. It portrayed two people, one clad in orange, and the other in green, engaged in an embrace. Though engaging and embracing, the two figures were still clearly distinct and still clearly represented their own particular traditions and cultures. The 700 people at this large meeting were then asked to find, and embrace, a person from 'the other' community.

As Ken watched 700 Protestants and Catholics embrace each other in the love of Christ, he realised that this was a sign of Ulster's future, that Christians should be the first people to embrace the changes they want to see in their country. This event filled all present with a new sense of hope in a bleak political and religious landscape. Although Ken Newell spoke these words on the radio in 1981, they prefigure a compelling reformulation of 'embrace' in the work of Miroslav Volf, whose 1995 article, 'A Vision of Embrace,' soon found its way into the peace-oriented discourse in Northern Ireland.

> In an embrace I open my arms to create space in myself for the other. Open arms are a sign that I do not want to be by myself only, an invitation for the other to come in and feel at home with me. In an embrace I also close my arms around the other. Closed arms are a sign that I want the other to become a part of me, the other enriches me. In a mutual embrace none remains the same because each enriches the other, yet both remain true to their genuine selves.

The day after Newell's radio address his phone rang. The caller was a young American, Greg Hendrickson, who asked for Ken's text. When Ken asked why, Greg disclosed that he was working as an intern for Fr Christy McCarthy at Clonard monastery, hoping to set up Bible studies and prayer meetings for people in the Renewal movement, Protestants and Catholics alike. Ken met Fr Christy a few days later. The two discussed the idea of a friendship-in-mission between Fitzroy and the Church of the Most Holy Redeemer. The Clonard-Fitzroy Fellowship began in principle, though at first they used the more alliterative 'Falls-Fitzroy Fellowship'.

Fr Christy was a generation older than Ken, but the two hit it off quite well, and their partnership gave renewed energy to the vision of cross-community Bible study first envisioned by McCarthy. Ken was completely taken with the priest's human vivacity and Christian grace. Ken later recalled that in Christy he believed God had provided the mentor and friend for the cross-community ministry to which he too believed himself called. But Christy's health was in a downward spiral by then, and he was in constant pain and confined to a wheelchair. He was to die about a year later, and many of the plans Ken and Christy had hoped to institute needed to be put on hold. Ken later recalled that he was hurt to learn of Christy's death only after the funeral. Ken wondered if another door for his ministry, which had seemed to open so unexpectedly and promisingly, would now close – like the friendship with Denis Newbury of St Malachy's back in south Belfast, which had looked so promising once but had not been sustained.

It took a little time for Clonard to re-position itself in regard to this cross-community work. The whole scene at Clonard was to change markedly with the arrival of Fr Gerry Reynolds in the autumn of 1983. We should take a few pages to discuss aspects of Gerry's life and thought before he came to Belfast.

Gerard Reynolds was born into a farming family in the parish of Mungret, a few miles west of Limerick city, in 1935. He was the second child in a family of four, one girl and three boys. The death of his father, Bartholomew, in 1941 at the age of 43 put a big burden on his mother, Mary Callaghan. Gerry remembers his mother's vibrant prayer life and her constant struggle to survive financially. Her faith and the strong support of neighbours enabled the family to cope. Two of his father's brothers, James and Gerard, were Redemptorist priests. Both worked for long periods in the Redemptorist community in Belfast. Mary, his father's only sister, became a Mercy Sister in Cork and was a big influence on Gerry until her death in 1969.

The first Protestant people Gerry came to know were among his mother's friends and customers: Miss Thompson, a Church of Ireland woman, and Mr Wood, a Baptist. They were regular visitors from the city to buy fresh eggs from the farm. Gerry remembers listening intently as a little boy to a discussion in the home kitchen on some question of faith between Mr Wood and John Callaghan, his mother's brother. Out of the fullness of his catechism knowledge Gerry intervened in the discussion, only to be told by his mother next day that little boys should be quiet when their elders are speaking!

Gerry received four years of his secondary education in St Munchin's College, Limerick and the final year in the Redemptorist St Clement's College, Limerick. He then joined the Redemptorist community and completed his novitiate formation in Athenry, Co Galway, making his first vows in September 1953. Having received his BA degree from University College Galway in 1956, he studied philosophy and theology in the Redemptorist seminary at Cluain Mhuire in Galway. His youngest brother, Pat, also joined the Redemptorists. His brother Michael took over the home farm, married and raised his six children there. His sister Noreen emigrated to England in the late 1950s and in 1961 married John Castle, an English Anglican. That decision created some tensions in the family but they were so completely overcome that John, still an Anglican, was best man at Michael's wedding in 1966. Family bonds were, and are, very important in Gerry's life.

The journey of faith for Gerry Reynolds has been guided by some powerful ideas and impressions that have come to him through important role models. First among those is Fr Sean O'Riordan, who for many years was the theology lecturer for those in formation at Cluain Mhuire. It was from Fr Sean that the young undergraduate would gain his first major insight about Protestants, who had not figured much in his early development. O'Riordan disclosed that he had many good conversations with Protestants in the north of Ireland, and that he had found so many of them had a great love for Jesus. Gerry later recalled that 'Fr Sean's words gave birth in me to a sense of kinship and communion in the love of Jesus with people of the Protestant traditions. He was only telling us the truth as he had come to know it in his visits to Belfast. I am grateful that he bore witness among us to the truth he had experienced. What Sean O'Riordan told us about Protestant people tallied with what we were hearing from our founder, St Alphonsus, in our Redemptorist formation:

To love Jesus Christ is the greatest work we can perform on earth; but it is a work and a gift we cannot have of ourselves; it must come to us from him, and he is ready to give it to those who ask him for it. ... He who loves the Lord is not content with just loving him; he will want to bring all to his love.

That was to be a sustaining vision for Gerry. Over the years, he grew ever more certain that Catholics and Protestants could meet one another in the love of our Lord Jesus Christ. But Gerry knew he must embody that love in his own life. The Rule of the Redemptorists had this reminder for Gerry and his colleagues: 'Their success in promoting the union of all Christians will be in proportion to their own earnest efforts to lead a life ever more in accord with the gospel.'

Gerry was ordained a priest in September 1960. During a short visit home after ordination he again met Miss Thompson, his mother's Church of Ireland friend. He wondered if she would like to receive his first blessing. The only way to know was to risk asking. He discovered she was utterly delighted to receive the blessing of the young priest, her friend's son. In ways like this, Gerry learned what right relationships between the disciples of Jesus might mean.

In the final year of his seminary formation, and in all the years since ordination, Gerry has been deeply influenced by the life and example of Pope John XXIII who was elected Bishop of Rome in October 1958. In the words of John Hewitt's poem 'Rome Sunday June 1960' which Gerry likes to quote, he has 'shared the blessing of that good Pope John'.

The Vatican Council, initiated by Pope John, led to a thorough review of life and renewal in the Catholic Church and in Gerry's own Redemptorist congregation. The Council deepened Gerry's commitment to proclaim in friendship and in word the message of plentiful redemption. He cherishes the Trinitarian formulation of that message and its emphasis on God's friendship in the Constitution on Divine Revelation. Pope John was for Gerry a witness to this divine friendship towards every human person:

It pleased God, in his goodness and wisdom, to reveal himself and to make known the mystery of his will. His will was that all should have access to the Father, through Christ, the Word made Flesh, in the Holy Spirit, and thus become sharers in the divine nature.

By this revelation, then, the invisible God, from the fullness of his love, addresses all people as his friends, and moves among them, in order to invite and receive them into his own company.

Another poem, 'A man named John,' published in the magazine *America* shortly after Pope John's death in 1963, keeps his memory and inspiration alive for Gerry:

'There was a man named John.' A prophet? Yes,
And greater than a prophet, if you mean
By prophet him who understands the times;
Or if you will, a man who finds the times
Significant, because he finds in them
The signs of times to come (whose fulfilment is
Only a matter of time). 'There was a man
Named John.' A simple and old-fashioned man
Who, when the fashion was suspicion and
Despair, with men damning their fellow men
Or fleeing them in fear, could dare to love
the worst of men. And even hope. 'There was
A man named John.' I know his voice is silent
Now, but the words he spoke give you and me
Reason to hope, reason to love. And come
What may, we know the Pentecostal Spirit
Stays with us still, prays in us still, for in
The desert of our times He breathed in John.'

In May 1962 Gerry joined the team of Redemptorist Publications in Dublin. Later in the 1960s he was involved in the founding of the Religious Press Association, an ecumenical endeavour bringing together Catholic, Church of Ireland and Presbyterian publishers. From 1969 to 1975 he worked with the Catholic Communications Institute and edited *Intercom*, a monthly pastoral magazine. At the first meeting of the Irish Council of Churches and the Irish Catholic Bishops in 1973, he

sat at lunch beside Rev Jim McEvoy, his Methodist neighbour in
Rathgar, Dublin where they both lived within a half-mile of one
another. Though they had lived so close for ten years, this was
their first meeting. An immediate friendship developed. They
both believed that inter-church meetings at national level would
mean little unless they were replicated at local level. Soon after-
wards, through their initiative, the Rathgar/Terenure Clergy
Fellowship came into being. It brought together local Methodist,
Church of Ireland, Presbyterian and Catholic clergy and has
done so almost every month since then. The fellowship has been
a source of blessing for the whole neighbourhood.

Gerry recalls one meeting in the early days of the Fellowship
which had a profound effect on him. Rev Robert Nelson, the
emeritus Rathgar Methodist minister, read a paper on his understanding of the Eucharist. When he had finished, Fr Alfie Tonge,
the Catholic parish priest of Terenure said, 'Robert, if that is
your understanding of the Eucharist, you are my soul brother.'
Jim McEvoy and Robert Nelson were the first of many
Methodist friends in Gerry's life. He sees the founder of his own
Redemptorist family as very similar in spirit to John Wesley, the
founder of the Methodists. Alphonsus de Liguori and John
Wesley were virtually contemporaries. Gerry recognises them
both as men of devotion and saints for all seasons.

After the publication of the Anglican Roman Catholic
International Commission (ARCIC) Agreed Statement on the
doctrine of the Eucharist in 1971, the two co-chairmen of ARCIC,
Henry McAdoo, Church of Ireland Archbishop of Dublin and
Alan Clarke, Roman Catholic Bishop of East Anglia, conducted
a day's conference in Dublin at the invitation of the Religious
Press Association. Gerry found great encouragement in that
conference. The ARCIC Agreed Statement on the Eucharist is for
him a powerful example of how the Spirit of God can lead us
from the polemical alienation of the past into a transformed relationship with one another. Working together in friendship,
prayer and dialogue, the two bishops and their commission had
reached a profound agreement in faith. Gerry believes that a key

element in the methodology of the commission can be replicated among the ordinary believers of the churches. That happens when people meet in friendship, leave aside the polemics of the past and speak to one another out of their living faith. By such unfettered dialogue about what the celebration of the Lord's Supper means to them, and aided by the ARCIC text, they can move towards agreement in faith. The reflection stimulated by the ARCIC achievement would continue in Gerry's life through all his years in Belfast.

Gerry Reynolds left Dublin in 1975 to become Rector of the Redemptorist Community in Limerick from 1975 to 1978. From 1978 to 1983, as a member of their community in Athenry, Co Galway, he preached parish missions and retreats throughout the West of Ireland. During those years he was deeply influenced and inspired by other people beyond the Redemptorist community. One of them was Charles de Foucauld, whose missionary charism touched his life through the Jesus Caritas Fraternity of Priests, with which Gerry has been involved since its establishment in Ireland in 1974. From de Foucauld he learned that what matters in the end is not success or failure but fidelity in the path into which one is called. It was the example of de Foucauld's life that enabled him to say to himself as he began his ministry in Belfast, 'Even if I have nothing to show for whatever years I spend here, that will be all right provided I'm faithful to the way in which God calls me.'

Perhaps the most important directly ecumenical influence on Gerry's life and work was Fr Paul Couturier, a person often referred to as the father of ecumenical prayer for the unity of Christians. He lived only sixty-three years, 1891-1953, yet he had a profound impact. Couturier was a priest in the diocese of Lyons, France. In the 1920s a large number of Russian Orthodox Christians settled there, having fled the communist revolution in their own country. Fr Paul's bishop asked him to welcome the Russians and help with their settlement. In due course he was to make some lasting friendships with the Russians. Their deep sense of spirituality caused him to realise the extent to which the various traditions in the church were impoverished through being cut off from each other for centuries. Couturier came to see that to end the churches' divisions and to revitalise the whole church, several changes of attitude must occur: acknowledgement by all churches of their own sins in causing and perpetuating divisions; converging prayer in all churches that they should work together toward the unity that Christ wants for them; respect for the freedom and integrity of all traditions, and that the larger churches not try to intimidate or swallow up the smaller ones. Couturier was the first to bring together Catholic, Orthodox and Protestants to pray together for each other and for the unity Christ wants for his church. Couturier gathered them in Lyons in the Church of the Family of Adoration (of which more below). When Fr Gerry was later to see Couturier's grave, the French friend who accompanied him said, 'Il etait un homme qui est venu de l'avenir' (He was a man who came out of the future).

Another large influence on Gerry's willingness to come to Belfast, and a very practical one, was his growing attachment to an international contemplative community, The Family of Adoration. The community had been founded in Paris, out of the social unrest of the so-called 'Revolution of 1848'. Theodolinde Dubouche, a young artist, gathered friends in a convent near Paris to pray for direction in those troubled times. Gradually, Theodolinde came to see that the way of peace was the essence of the gospel, and that she and her friends were called to a life of loving and adoring God and of a loving presence among people in need. The Family of Adoration came to Belfast in 1980 at the invitation of Dr Philbin, Bishop of Down and Connor. They chose a house on the Falls Road and came to live there during the hunger strike riots in 1981, when buses and cars were often burning not far from their front door. Their chapel has been a centre of prayer and peace ever since. Their example of being a living and loving presence in the midst of strife – of incarnating a gospel witness – was a powerful influence on Gerry Reynolds.

Finally, in many ways the friendship between Ken Newell and Gerry Reynolds is, at least for Gerry, inspired by the friendship of Marc Boegner, a pastor in the French Reformed Church and Giovanni Montini, later to be Pope Paul VI. If one goes on a pilgrimage to Jerusalem, one finds a prayer garden near to Gethsemene, dedicated to the friendship between Boegner and Montini. During his time in Jerusalem, at the Tantur Ecumenical Institute in the late 1980s, Gerry often went to that garden to think and pray. A quote from Boegner out of that friendship has become a virtual motto for Gerry Reynolds' life: 'The church must be Catholic or it will not be the church at all. The believer must be Protestant or he or she will not be a believer at all.' In sum, the beliefs that guided Gerry as he came to minister in Belfast can be worked out of Boegner's formulation. Every church must be 'Catholic' – open to all people and to all truth, never sectarian or petty, never turned in on itself, but rather in communion with all churches throughout the world. Every believer must be 'Protestant', in whatever tradition, and must make his or her own personal protestation of faith in Christ as Saviour and Lord. Belief must be personal and from the heart. Each one makes his or her own act of faith. No one else can make it for them.

I hope that the above few pages help to get to know the background and the thinking of the man who Fr George Wadding, Rector of Clonard, invited to come to Belfast in the summer of 1983, following the death of Christy McCarthy. Fr Gerry had high expectations for his new assignment, his first in Northern Ireland. But, as he later told me, he had no idea that it would lead him into the paths of service that it did, or of the recognition which the Pax Christi award would bestow.

CHAPTER THREE

The Clonard-Fitzroy Fellowship

After Christy McCarthy's death in the late summer of 1983, Ken Newell was concerned about what the future might hold for the fledgling relationship between Fitzroy Presbyterian Church and Clonard monastery. Ken had pinned a great deal of hope on that partnership for co-operative mission, and he was very eager to know where he and his people stood with the priests and brothers at Clonard.

Gerry Reynolds, for his part, was fully aware of how much he had to learn in local terms to translate his vocation of reconciliation into practical reality. While he was mindful of and grateful for the considerable contribution that people from the Charismatic Renewal and from Moral Re-Armament had made with Fr Christy, Gerry wanted his ministry to proceed along the lines of what he calls 'a radical orthodoxy', drawing from the deepest roots of the Christian tradition. Moreover, as we have seen above, Gerry always filtered his Catholic ideas through a thorough consciousness of ecumenical yearning, in the manner of Paul Couturier.

There were other initial impressions made in Gerry Reynolds' mind in those early weeks of his new life in Belfast. For example, he had a long conversation with Fr Alec Reid, a fellow Redemptorist priest at Clonard. He will figure largely in a later chapter, but enough for now to say that Gerry was given, early on, a compelling case from Alec that the Catholic vocation to peace in Northern Ireland should have a political dimension as well as a churchly dimension. Further, to pursue that dual vocation, Reid insisted, peacemakers must be open to, and in dialogue with, all parties involved in religious and social strife in

Northern Ireland. Another member of the Clonard community, Brother Hugh Murray, also added a great insight for Gerry's orientation to west Belfast. Brother Hugh, already almost eighty years of age when Gerry met him, had lived and grown up in the Clonard area, and had sung in the Clonard choir as a boy. During his long life of service, Hugh had worked in the Redemptorist mission in the Philippines, and then in various communities in Ireland. When Gerry met Hugh he was twenty years back in Belfast. As Gerry later recalled, Brother Hugh took him up to the third floor of the Monastery, where one can look out over the Peace Line to the Protestant Shankill Road.

> Out of his many memories he was explaining the situation to me as only a local man can. He pointed out the street off the Shankill where he visits his friend, a Presbyterian woman as old as himself. She comes to see him at the monastery with her home help, a Church of Ireland woman, whose son, a UDA man, was doing a long sentence in Long Kesh prison. Brother Hugh carries all the people of the Shankill and the Falls in his heart. He knows their pain and understands their fears. Looking out over their homes he said to me, 'They are all the same people – for generations the same factory hooters ruled their lives, calling them to the mills. They were all exploited and their differences were exaggerated to keep them divided. Neither group got a fair share of the wealth they created.' From the humble and gentle spirit of Brother Hugh I learned something of God's compassion and care for his people in the Shankill and the Falls.

Further, from outside the Clonard community came another initial impression for the priest from Limerick. Because it is important for us to hear Ken and Gerry in their own voices as much as possible, let's listen to the way Gerry told a story of a chance encounter with a Protestant man along the Shankill.

> In September 1983, when I was less than a month in Belfast, I walked along the Shankill Road for the first time, dressed as a clergyman, but in grey. In the Community Information Centre I met an elderly man named George. 'You're up from the Free State, Padre,' he said. 'Yes,' said I. 'And where are you ministering?' 'Not very far away, over the wall at

Clonard church.' The game was up. He knew who I was then, but we talked at length. Before parting I asked him, 'Have you any advice for me as a newcomer to Belfast?' His answer still rings in my memory: 'You clergy will have to get together to bring the church to the people again.'

It was with these various thoughts on his mind and heart that Fr Gerry Reynolds invited Rev Ken Newell to lunch shortly after Easter in 1984. When walking in the garden on the Clonard grounds, the Angelus Bell rang. Gerry said, 'Ken, there's the Angelus.' Ken answered, 'Gerry, what's the Angelus?' Gerry later told me that he thought Ken actually knew what it was but that he wanted to hear Gerry's explanation. He later told me he'd probably said something like: 'It is time to ponder God's coming to be with us in human history through Jesus and his Spirit, and to ponder also Mary's exemplary response to God's initiative and call.' Gerry recalls that moment as a time of confirmation he should go forward in faith with Ken and pick up the threads of co-operation left by Fr Christy.

Gerry's friendship with Ken would indeed work out well and have great consequences, but in a certain way he didn't have much choice but to go ahead with Ken. It was not necessarily the most obvious thing to do for a Catholic community rooted in working-class west Belfast to associate with Fitzroy Presbyterian Church, a largely middle-class congregation in the university section of south Belfast. In view of the differences in physical and social location, the fact of the Clonard-Fitzroy Fellowship's success is all the more remarkable. Years later, I sat with Gerry in his room on the third floor of the Clonard building, seeing much the same view of the Peace Line and the Shankill Road as he had shared with Brother Hugh two decades earlier. I asked him about the logic of the relationship with Fitzroy. While his answer was clearly affirmative as to the rightness of that friendship, Gerry affirmed that he was also called to have a particular ministry to the Falls-Shankill area. In due course, Gerry became a member of the Cornerstone Community, an inter-faith centre of Methodist foundation which has,

since 1982, served as a place of prayer and sanctuary at the interface between the Falls and the Shankill. It had grown out of an
inter-church prayer meeting that had met in Clonard since the
mid-1970s. In a later chapter we will meet Rev Sam Burch, a
Methodist minister whose denomination seconded him in 1986
to lead the Cornerstone Community.

The Clonard-Fitzroy Fellowship was to be successful and it
never bogged down along geographic or class lines. In fact, most
people involved in the Fellowship agree that issues of differences in educational attainment and social class did not unduly
intrude on their working together for mutual understanding
and reconciliation. Those involved in the Fellowship were sin-
cere, dedicated Christians who gave little if any attention to con-
tingent matters that might divide others. At the same time, some
people I interviewed told me that they were aware, at first, that
more people from Fitzroy than Clonard were likely to be university graduates, doctors and lawyers. But, the point they all em-
phasised insofar as they talked about class at all was that as
friendships developed in their common mission, these Christian
friends quickly and easily overcame other possible impedi-
ments. For them, it was an important point to stress, that while
one did initially notice class differences, the liberating power of
the gospel brought the Clonard and Fitzroy people together in a
purposeful and exciting way.

We should mention near the beginning of our discussion of
the Fellowship that relatively few members of the two congregations participated in its life. Several people important to the
vocation of reconciliation in the two congregations asked that I
stress two points here: that the Clonard-Fitzroy Fellowship was
'a wee group', and that there were other examples of churches
doing worthwhile cross-community work that did not receive
the public acclaim of their group. This writer found such self-
effacing protestations to be fully consistent with the genuine
Christian qualities of the clergy and people involved.

Gerry and Ken agreed early on that they should have a long-
term view and not ask too much too soon of their peoples in the

group. This proved to be wise foresight, as events have shown. The two comrades encouraged the development and deepening of care and personal friendships among their people, hoping and believing that in due course reconciliation between the two communities could be achieved. Over the initial six or seven years, the Fellowship was mostly centred on Bible study and prayer together, along with occasional events such as visits to each other's churches. Moreover, the lay people could see and feel the high regard and care the two clergy accorded each other, and the people drew strength from that. There were also a few events of high drama that gave members in the Fellowship a sense of élan and purpose. For example, the Fellowship supported a meeting at Fitzroy Church in 1986 that all those present would not forget, and would also bind them together in the memory of a common achievement.

Ken, along with a few of his Presbyterian colleagues, had entertained the hope that his own denomination would awaken to a divine vocation in Northern Ireland to become an instrument of peace and reconciliation. But that required building some bridges of dialogue between Presbyterians and Roman Catholics and very few existed, certainly none with a high public profile. With the help of his colleagues and the backing of three former Moderators of the Presbyterian Church in Ireland, a fringe meeting was organised in June 1983, during the week of the General Assembly in Dublin. The speakers were Dr Alan Flavelle, Minister of Lowe Memorial Presbyterian Church, Belfast, and probably the most influential and respected evangelical thinker of his day, and Dr Cahal Daly, Catholic Bishop of Down and Connor, whose concern to reach out to Protestants was a distinguishing feature of his ministry in Belfast. The meeting was held on a cold, wind-swept Wednesday evening in Abbey Presbyterian Church, close to the centre of Dublin. As the news of the event percolated through the conversations of the Assembly, some expressed reservations about the wisdom of holding it; when the weather took a turn for the worse, others wondered if anyone would turn up. As the evening unfolded the response was found to be greater than anyone anticipated: about 200 people packed into one of the large halls of the Abbey Church, among them 50 local Catholics from the Dublin area and about 150 Presbyterian ministers and elders who were delegates at the Assembly. They listened with rapt attention as both speakers, flanked by the ex-Moderators of the church, demonstrated from the scriptures that followers of Jesus Christ have a clear responsibility to be instruments of God's peace in situations of social conflict and inter-community violence. Something special happened that evening in the hearts of some of those present. But there was more to be done if progress was to be sustained.

Ken, and those involved in planning this event, were aware that it was one thing to organise such a ground-breaking initiative in the milder climate of Dublin, Ireland's capital city; it would require a lot of courage to bring it north to the Protestant heartland in Belfast. But the opportunity presented itself in 1986 in association with the evangelistic event 'There is Hope'. Ken had been involved with the leaders of this initiative and they were keen to cross the traditional religious barriers that block the impact of sharing the gospel with the total northern Irish community. As part of that initiative Ken invited to Fitzroy, with the permission of his elders, the Presbyterian Moderator for the year, Rev Dr Robert Dickinson, and Dr Cahal Daly, the Catholic Bishop of Down and Connor. Dr Dickinson was well-known for his conservative evangelical theological beliefs and his opposition to the World Council of Churches. Dr Daly's unrelenting criticism of the violence of the IRA had won him much respect within the Catholic and the wider Protestant community. This meeting, as far as one knows, was the first time in Northern Ireland, and perhaps in Ireland, that a serving Presbyterian Moderator and Catholic Bishop spoke together in the same church and shared their distinct perspectives on the theme of Christ as the source of hope for all people.

It was a public event that few of those who attended will ever forget. As the evening drew near for the meeting, pressure mounted. Dozens of policemen and soldiers in their Landrovers had to protect the building and guarantee free access to the event for all who desired to attend. Rev Ian Paisley and about 200 of his fundamentalist supporters surrounded the church in protest. Many of the pickets were hostile and verbally abusive towards those making their way into the church.

As the service got underway and the congregation sang hymns, protesters inside began to disrupt proceedings. As Dr Dickinson began to speak he was interrupted by repeated shouting; when Bishop Daly spoke, one protester grabbed hold of the Communion Table in front of the pulpit and screamed 'Antichrist'. As the protesters began to disrupt the service some were escorted from the building by the ushers of Fitzroy while the more tenacious were removed by the police. About twelve were shown the door.

Despite all that was happening, Ken was conscious of a strong sense of God's presence. Dozens of those from a fundamentalist perspective who came into the service in very critical attitude were apparently touched by the genuineness of the occasion. While many of those present may have shared the theological and political views of the protesters, they were perhaps embarrassed by the aggressive language and disruptive behaviour. On their way out of the service, Ken overheard conversations in which some people expressed their annoyance and anger directly to the protestors about the way they had acted. Several weeks later Ken received a letter from a young Presbyterian theological student who had been angry that the event should take place at all. However, he had decided, out of curiosity, to attend. Having sat through the evening and watched, listened and thought for himself, he wrote, 'I came to Fitzroy in a very angry mood, but as I sat there listening to the speakers, I realised that I had attitudes that needed to be touched by the grace of Christ and changed. Please God the changes that started in me that night will continue in the years to come.'

Ken later recalled: 'It was an astonishing night. A few days before it, I was coming under intense pressure to cancel the event. I talked over with my wife Val the risks involved to people and property. But her words of encouragement to me are still as clear today as they were then: "Ken, if we don't do it now, we'll never do it." I took a deep breath, thanked God for Val's constant support, and settled in my mind to face with determination and faith whatever lay ahead.' He also notes that 'The fact that this meeting took place at all spoke volumes about the open-mindedness of Fitzroy's Kirk Session, and in particular the involvement of the Clerk of Session, Denis Boyd, and several other elders who acted as ushers. It also highlighted the courage and determination of the two eminent speakers and the unwillingness of peacemakers in Northern Ireland to yield to the threats and intimidation of those who have nothing to offer in building a better future for our people.'

The consequences of that remarkable evening were several. It deepened the desire of those in Fitzroy committed to the ministry of reconciliation and peacemaking to repeat the event. Several similar events involving Presbyterian Moderators and theologians, and Catholic bishops and cardinals have taken place in the intervening years. There was a reaction among some fundamentalist Christians in Northern Ireland to such a highly publicised disruption of a church service. Captured on TV, the protesters' ugly images did nothing to commend their point of view. The level of public protest at such events dropped noticeably in the years that followed. The members of the Clonard-Fitzroy Fellowship felt a huge surge of encouragement and inspiration in seeing leaders who were prepared to take risks for peace. Many of them, especially the Clonard people, later told me that such events, and the shared memory of them, empowered them to keep walking the pathway of peace during the dark and bitter days of the 1980s and 1990s.

It is important to recall that the initial focus of the Fellowship – Bible study and prayer – was vital to the developing trust between the two congregations. The Bible gave a common point of reference. As they reflected on the scriptures they could share their own stories which often contained pain, resentment, exclusion and discrimination. Surrounding the meetings, of course, the usual cycles of life occurred – birth, death, marriage, illness – in which Fellowship members could sympathise. Several people told me that the breakthrough moment for them happened when a member of 'the other' church visited them in the hospital or came to pay respects for a loved one who had died. When a group like the Clonard-Fitzroy Fellowship begins to function well, it becomes a setting in which trust is plighted and expected, and in which a person can express one's true self. The members are not so much people who see big visions or dream huge dreams. Rather, they are practical Christians with a personal conviction about trying to do whatever they can to bring peace and reconciliation in their divided society. So, for example, here is a short testimony from a self-proclaimed 'ordinary' person. Sheila McNeill, a Fitzroy member of the Fellowship, was asked by Fr Gerry to write one typescript page for *Reality*, the monthly magazine of the Redemptorist order.

I am an ordinary middle-class Protestant. I am thirty-three years old, and I work as a part-time physiotherapist. I am married with two small children. I grew up unaffected directly by the Troubles, and perhaps like many others from both communities I became immune to the sectarianism that has polluted our society, not only in the acts of violence but in the attitudes of ordinary people like me

After I graduated in 1984 I lived in England for three years and in Israel for one year before returning to Belfast. Looking at Northern Ireland from outside I realised just how divided the society was in which I grew up. I remember the impact the Enniskillen bomb had on the people in Jerusalem and I was humbled that people all over the world were affected by such a tragedy in my little country.

When I came back to Belfast I sought out a church where there was some sort of reconciliation work going on. That search led me to Fitzroy Presbyterian Church where the Rev Ken Newell actively promoted reconciliation. I soon joined the Clonard/Fitzroy Reconciliation Group and I have enjoyed the various discussions held. I have been impressed by people within the group who have lived through discrimination or intimidation at work, or who have seen members of their family imprisoned, and yet seek the road of reconciliation instead of retaliation. I believe that the experience of Protestant/Roman Catholic reconciliation has made me more aware of other areas of painful division: between classes, abilities and sexes. My hope is that in developing a heart for one area of human reconciliation we can change in other areas towards God's command that we love one another.

Marie McMullan, a Clonard member, grew up in the Falls Road area, and has been a member of the Fellowship from the beginning. In the context of the Troubles she was motivated to action in a practical way. She says, 'It's easy to feel bitter about what's happened in Northern Ireland since 1969. But you have to work at getting to know the other religions. It doesn't just happen.' And, in getting to know each other, people come to know the special gift or insight another might have. For example, Jim Stewart, a Clonard Catholic, has a special role in the group. Jim had been born and raised as a Protestant but became a Catholic when he married. His special insight gives him the unique role of interpreting each community to the other. The words of this quiet and gentle man are much respected. Sandra Rutherford, a college teacher, is a Fitzroy member of the Fellowship. Like many other middle-class Protestants, Sandra grew up in an area of Ulster where there were few Catholics in her life. But, like many others committed to reconciliation, Sandra's experience with Catholics overseas made her eager to explore possibilities of friendships with Catholics once she came home to Ireland from Africa. The Clonard-Fitzroy Fellowship Bible studies allowed her to develop trusting friendships with Catholics, friendships that would sustain her through a particularly difficult period. Writing for the Redemptorist magazine in 2000:

> I was ill with cancer about eight years ago, and it was a pretty bad prognosis. At that time the Clonard people prayed for me and I believe I'm here now because of their prayers. I remember the first chemotherapy session I had. I was feeling very nervous. I remembered that there was a Mass being said

at that exact time for me in Clonard, and it gave me a real
sense of peace, and helped me through it all. Our traditions
are different in some ways, but one of the things I have come
to admire on the Clonard side is the faithfulness of prayer.

As I interviewed many people at Clonard and Fitzroy, and
read the minutes of the committee on the Fitzroy side, the name
of one family kept coming up: the Rutherfords. The Fitzroy and
Clonard people alike sing the praises of the Rutherfords, and
point to them as people who have made an essential difference.
The towering figure, in both physical and moral stature, is
William Rutherford, now a retired surgeon living in Belfast.
Also, a genuine grassroots leader who quietly gets a great deal
done is his daughter-in-law, Sandra Rutherford (mentioned
above). While surely many people have contributed to the suc-
cess of the Clonard-Fitzroy Fellowship, all are agreed that only
Ken and Gerry themselves are of more importance that the
Rutherfords.

William Rutherford was, in his medical role, well known to
the Catholic people of west Belfast because of his leadership in
seeing that Catholics, both patients and staff, received equal
treatment at the Royal Victoria Hospital in the Falls Road, not
far from Clonard monastery. Some people think that William
looks like a prophet and many others regard his actions and
words as prophetic. For example, there was an occasion when
the Clonard-Fitzroy Fellowship visited Ballynafeigh Orange
Hall in order to learn directly about Orangeism, its values, its
beliefs and the struggles it sees itself facing. About 40 members
of the group crowded into a small room where a well-known
local Orangeman explained the history of the Order. As the conversations and questions flowed backwards and forwards,
William spoke some important words. The term 'parity of esteem' had recently been coined. It referred to the hoped-for
change of attitudes in which the two traditions in Northern
Ireland would be treated and regarded as equally worthy and
valuable. However, Dr Rutherford thought 'parity of esteem'
too limiting because it highlighted what one might feel deprived

of, such as social and political entitlements. Rather, Rutherford wanted to concentrate on the Christian values of love and respect, which led him to try a new term, 'the generosity of esteem'. Such attitudes would characterise his wide-ranging influence on people and events.

Sandra Rutherford is an equally outstanding example of how far the work of an ordinary person might have impact. She is much respected by the Clonard members of the Fellowship for her many acts of gentle acceptance and deep kindness, and for what they call her 'down-to-earth' style of interaction. Yet, she is also a woman of ideas who is very willing to share them in the right place and way. For Sandra, an important new lesson learned in the Fellowship was the awareness that both communities can minister to each other. This was at first led by the clergy, when she realised that Gerry was as much a minister to her as Ken; and then by the laity, when members of each church cared for the other. Sandra put some of this into words in 1992 when the Clonard-Fitzroy people had a weekend together at Corrymeela, the well-known residential reconciliation centre on the north Antrim coast:

> At one early meeting I was sharing in a small group how my spiritual life had become dry. Fr Gerry Reynolds said, 'Let your roots go deep down into the soil of God's marvellous love.' He reminded me of the story of Jesus as the vine, that we are the branches, and that we can't do anything if we are not rooted in him. Gerry had ministered to me. At the beginning of the Fellowship we didn't often go to each other's churches. It was difficult for some of the Presbyterian members, and especially difficult to attend Mass. However, we soon found that we were very welcome when we did go. Ken, our minister, was soon asked to preach, and everyone stood and clapped. The next time a Methodist minister preached and again everyone stood and clapped. At the third time when someone else was being applauded Ken realised what it meant, that it hadn't been the brilliance of his sermon, but that all of us Protestants were very welcome.
>
> We at Fitzroy had difficulty in reciprocating this welcome. After a few visits from Clonard folk, and with permis-

sion of the elders, some one from Clonard was asked to read
from the Bible. On the next visit, one was asked to pray
(though some Fitzroy people wanted to check to see if the
prayer was all right). Very gradually over the years we now
have the position where folks from Clonard can preach and
take full part in our services.

But, communion evidences the real pain of separation. A
discussion of *One Bread One Body* was led by Paul Symonds,
the priest who is delegated by his bishop to give permission
for Christians of other traditions to receive communion in the
Roman Catholic Church on special occasions. He said he almost always said yes. I have had a difficulty in knowing
what to do at Clonard. The last time I was there, the priest's
words 'take, eat, *all* of you' helped me go forward and receive. I believed it was Jesus calling us to his table.

Karl Rahner says that the church of the future will be
made up of those who have struggled against their environ-
ment in order to reach a personally clear and explicitly responsible decision of faith. Reconciliation within our own
denomination to those with whom we disagree is difficult. It
is a journey many of us find hard to start.

While the Bible studies had been the backbone of the initial
development for the Clonard-Fitzroy Fellowship, the group's
natural maturation by about 1990 allowed it to envision moving
to new areas of learning and ministry. At this time there was
agreement about the name change. Early on, some Presbyterians
at Fitzroy may have been uneasy about designating a Catholic
church in the group's name, preferring a geographical area. But,
by 1990, the Presbyterian members of the Fellowship wanted to
go further and deeper with their Catholic friends, and the non-
Fellowship members at Fitzroy were getting used to the fact of
Catholics being around and about in Fitzroy, so the use of
Clonard instead of Falls in the group name was easily accepted.
The Catholic members of the Fellowship were also glad for the
name change that would now designate the church where they
belonged, not just the area of the city where it was located. This
was especially true for those Clonard church people who actually
did not live on the Falls Road.

Gerry wrote a mission statement for the newly-named Clonard-Fitzroy Fellowship, though it reads like a description of what had already been going on: the Fellowship was 'to promote contact, mutual understanding, respect and common witness'. In addition to the initial focus on Bible study, the fellowship was to develop 'as a school of spirituality where each can learn from the other tradition; as an organiser of reconciliation services for the larger congregations in Clonard and Fitzroy; as a forum for genuine dialogue between the conflicting political loyalties; as a witness to other Catholic and Protestant congregations to the value of such a group; as an explorer quietly searching for the reconciling church that is coming to be; as a gathering of friends who are able to socialise together and enjoy one another's Irish and Scottish cultures.'

With this refocused vision and new energy, the Fellowship began to organise a year's programme in terms of themes. For example, in 1991-92, the theme was 'Men, Women and God,' with sessions on mixed marriage, homosexuality, family planning and abortion. In 1992-93 the theme was 'The Mission of the Church,' with sessions to analyse worship in both churches and others to discuss with both Unionist and Nationalist politicians how their Christian faith might have political impact. These events were always in addition to the regular activities: a St Patrick's Day party, a Christmas carol service and supper, common worship during the week of Christian unity in January, and a weekend away together.

One of the trips taken by the Fellowship was to the St Joseph's Carmelite Monastery at Malahide, just outside Dublin, in the Republic of Ireland. The way had been paved by the redoubtable William Rutherford. On St Patrick's Day, 1996, he had given a talk to the sisters on the spirituality of St Patrick and how he could be shared by all Irish Christians, Protestants as much as Catholics. The prioress of St Joseph's, Sr Teresa, wrote to Ken Newell to report her community's great delight with the presentation of William Rutherford. She also asked Ken to come to preach on 9 June 1996, which was the feast of St Columba of

Derry. Ken did go on that day along with members of the Clonard-Fitzroy Fellowship. It was a memorable day for all: for the Protestants it may have been the first time in a Catholic church in the Republic; for the Catholics in the Fellowship is was an affirmation of their tradition; for the sisters of the monastery it was the first time most of them had worshipped with Protestants at all, never mind going over the top with the preacher being a Presbyterian from Belfast!

The various events held under the auspices of the Clonard-Fitzroy Fellowship are typically sombre, thought-provoking and challenging. But some are just good fun. Most often the St Patrick's Day party (*céilidh*, in Irish) is an evening of good fellowship, gaiety and laughter (known as *crack*). All serious subjects are left outside the hall, whether it is the alternate-year sites at Clonard or Fitzroy. There is lots of good food, singing and dancing as people from both traditions celebrate what they do, or might, hold in common. But, their very first St Patrick's evening together nearly didn't happen. On 19 March 1988 the people of the Fellowship had planned to have their first *céilidh* in Fitzroy's Alexander Hall. Between the planning and the event, however, there occurred the murders of IRA people in Gibraltar and those of the two British corporals at Milltown Cemetery in Belfast. Many people told me of their feeling numbed by seeing the pictures on television (we will return to these events in another chapter). The tension and fear felt in west Belfast was tangible. Some people from Clonard did not feel safe going to the party in south Belfast that night. But most of the Clonard people did not want to disappoint their Protestant friends, so they gathered their courage and drove down to University Street. The Clonard people brought with them four girls from the group called The McCoy Dancers. Fr Gerry later interviewed the girls for his newspaper column in *The Irish News*, calling their story 'a simple joy from a sad month'.

> We were asked to come and do an Irish dancing display. To be honest, we thought it was going to be a waste of a Saturday night. However, it was one of the few times when

all four of us felt we were really appreciated for what we did. Due to the trouble that day, we were apprehensive going. However, we got a fantastic welcome. People were warm and interested. They asked questions about our costumes and the dances we did. We were asked to demonstrate various céilidh dances and found that everyone wanted to join in. This surprised but pleased us. By the end of the night we felt that we had made a real contribution to inter-community relationships. It made us all question our attitudes and wonder just what the political issues that are tearing our country apart are trying to achieve. We want to thank everyone for the warm and friendly reception and for proving to us that Irish dancing is appreciated right across the religious divide. We are sad that it is not a larger part of life in the whole community.

In 1995 the hilarity at the St Patrick's Day *céilidh* reached a new high (or comic low) never before known. Sandra Rutherford, with help from a few co-conspirators, wrote a song for Gerry Reynolds' 60th birthday. The Fitzroy people sang it to the tune of the American Civil War anthem, 'The Battle Hymn of the Republic.' (North American readers may not know that a 'gerry can' is used to carry gasoline.)

Gerry Can
Father Gerry wants to bring peace to all men and to this end
He has talked with many folk and met with Presidents
But has not yet had an audience with his holiness the Pope
Though for that there is some hope.
Gerry, Gerry, he can do it
Gerry, Gerry, he can do it
Gerry, Gerry, he can do it
With his feet planted firmly in the clouds.

For organising services in Christian Unity Week
We had to look to Gerry to tell us when to speak
He told us we must all share in planning what to do
He said to us 'It all depends on you.'
Gerry, Gerry, we can do it
Gerry, Gerry, we can do it
Gerry, Gerry, we can do it
With our feet planted firmly on the ground.

Father Gerry we all love you and just would like to say
Don't worry about the passing years
          and hair that's turning grey
We know that you have more to do in this very needy place
And you can do it with God's grace.
Gerry, Gerry, God can do it
Gerry, Gerry, God can do it
Gerry, Gerry, God can do it
With your life resting firmly in His hand.

The combination of serious purpose and genuine fun for the Clonard-Fitzroy Fellowship was realised in another trip to the Republic, this time in 1993. The Fellowship responded to an invitation from Mary Robinson, President of the Republic, who wanted to honour them for their work for peace and reconciliation. They were very grateful that President Robinson met and prayed with them. For both Protestants and Catholics from Belfast, in the British province of Northern Ireland, it was a moving and memorable experience in exploring the Irish dimension to their lives.

One of the main occasions for reconciliatory activity for the Fellowship was the annual reconciliation services, held alternately at Fitzroy Presbyterian Church or at The Church of the Most Holy Redeemer. The typical pattern would be to sponsor a service on the first Sunday of Advent at one church, then another at the other church in January, during the Universal Week of Prayer for Unity. Because these services are so important to the life of the Fellowship and to its mission, we should try to get a feel for what actually goes on in them. For example, in 1988 the annual reconciliation service was held on Advent Sunday (November 27th) at Fitzroy. First, we should mention the notice that announced the service in the bulletins, in which people were invited to 'come and dedicate yourself again to making peace and to prepare your heart for Christmas'. Catholic participants must have been a bit surprised to note a custom of evangelical Protestantism that while the service would start at 7:00pm, there would be singing from 6:45! Then, as to the service, Ken Newell, the host pastor, welcomed everyone and called all to worship. Gerry Reynolds then prayed:

At my ordination, 25 September 1960, with my mother Mary Reynolds, my sister Noreen, and brothers Mike and Pat CSsR.

Walking with Fr Alec Reid in the monastery garden,
with Clonard church in the background.

*Ken Newell, Gerry Reynolds and Sam Burch in Lisburn, September 1994,
after meeting with members of the Ulster Democratic Party
and some of the UDA leadership.*

Canon Barry Dodds, Rector, St Michael's Church of Ireland parish, Shankill Road, Dalai Lama, Gerry Reynolds at the Belfast Peace Line Reception for the Dalai Lama, October 2000.

At Carrickfergus during the 2004 parish mission with unity pilgrims from Clonard and from the Catholic parish before dividing up to join the Morning Service in local Protestant churches.

Gerry and Ken with the Pax Christi award, November 1999.

Opposite:
President Mary McAleese visits Clonard, June 2003

Jim Stewart and Margaret Duffy, long-time Clonard members of the Fellowship with Fitzroy

At the 25th anniversary dinner in St John's Presbyterian Church Hall, Newtownbreda, Belfast in January 2001: (left to right) Jennie (daughter), Renee Ritchie (Val's mum), Siobhan (daughter-in-law), Val, Ken, Tim (son).

Sandra and James Rutherford

Opposite:

The Professors, Staff and Ministry Students of the Presbyterian Church's Assembly's College, Belfast. In this 1966-67 session, Ken Newell is in the second row, sixth from the right.

The visit of Archbishop Desmond Tutu to Fitzroy in October 1998.
Left to right: Jonathan Bradford (USA), Graeme Fowles (Youth Leader),
Dr Tutu, Ken, and Mary Seeger (USA Youth Volunteer).

Opposite:
Kirk Session, Fitzroy Presbyterian Church, 1984
Back row: P. Mateer, N. McConnell, L. Watson, A. Patterson, Miss J. P.
Gamble, B. Potter, R. Davidson, J. Lemon, P. McElroy, J. Malcomson,
J. Currie.
Middle row: V. Hagans, S. Rutherford, W. Watson, W. Flack, Rev Prof J. R.
Boyd, W. E. Dornan, W. Rutherford, H. Rutherford, F. H. S. Bell,
W. McCrum.
Front row: Miss M. Duncan, D. I. Wilson, J. H. McCollum,
Rev J. Brackenridge, D. A. Boyd, Rev K. N. E. Newell, T. W. S. Armstrong,
Rev R. E. Alexander, J. F. Jenkins, Miss R. Pelan

Val and Ken in Mount Stewart Estate, Greyabbey, Co Down, in August 2001

Monday 7 June 2004: Ken at the Reception on the Opening Night of the General Assembly with (l to r) Audrey Kerr (sister), Val (wife), Jennie (daughter) and Tim (son).

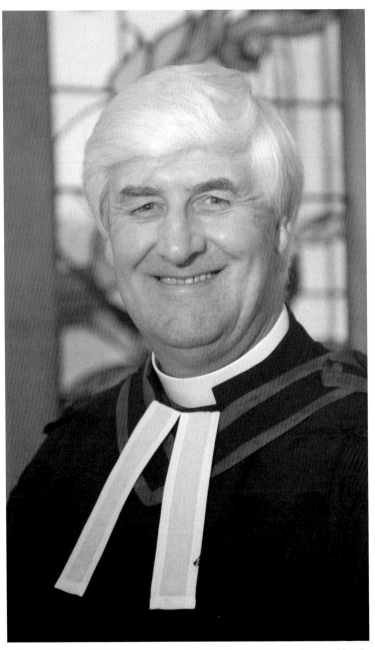

Ken on the eve of his inauguration as Moderator of the General Assembly of the Presbyrterian Church in Ireland on 7 June 2004.

Lord Jesus, we remember that when you prayed for your disciples the night before going to the cross, you also said, 'I pray not only for them, but also for those who believe in me because of their message. I pray that they may be one in the Father. May they be in us, just as you are in me and I am in you. May they be one so that the world may believe that you sent me.' Oh Jesus, pray again your prayer for us tonight, and make us a blessing to all among whom we live. We ask this in your name. Amen.

Then, after the Lord's Prayer, some Bible readings and a unison saying of the Apostle's Creed, four members of the Clonard-Fitzroy Fellowship led the congregation in the prayers of thanksgiving and intercession that had been written by William Rutherford:

Lord God, our Father, we thank you for giving us such a beautiful country to live in, with its mountains and valleys, its lakes and rivers, its green fields and varied coastline. We thank you for all the different people who have come here wherever they may have come from and whatever their original intentions. We thank you for all the different strands of our culture. We give thanks for St Patrick who brought the knowledge of your love to this land, and for all those since his time who have built up the faith and devotion to your church. We thank you that even today, when in many countries people have abandoned their Christian beliefs, there are still many in this land who love you and want to follow and serve you. We thank you for all the enrichment we have experienced by the members of different branches of your church coming closer together, trying to understand you better and to learn from each other. We thank you for the joy of celebrating together. We thank you for Advent, for the approach of Christmas, for all the messages and tokens of love that will be exchanged at this time.

Lord, we pray for our country, for all its people, North and South. We pray especially for the unemployed, for all who feel that they are shut out from sharing in the good things of life, who see no hope of ever owning a house or a car and who feel hurt and insulted by the flaunting of wealth and power on our television screens. Lord, show us the way to allow every citizen to make some contribution towards the life and wealth of our society. We pray for employers and for trade unions that they may find ways of distributing the job opportunities that exist fairly between our communities and sexes.

We remember the terrible events that have taken place in this past year. We remember the shootings in Milltown Cemetery and the killing of the soldiers a few days later. We remember Gibraltar, the first shock and all the subsequent pain through the days of the inquest. We remember the bombing of the soldiers' bus near Omagh, and all the other killings that have brought so much agony to so many people. Lord, have mercy on us all. God of comfort, draw near to all who have been bereaved.

We pray for all in our country who are dominated by hate and by bitterness. Oh Jesus, you are the saviour, the liberator. Free them from their bonds. We pray for those who have been drawn into paramilitary activity, who, to advance their cause, are prepared to rob and shoot and bomb and carry out terrible atrocities. We pray also for those who will not do such things themselves, but will give support to those who do. We do not find it easy to pray for them, but we know that it is your wish that we should do so, and we remember your prayer for those who crucified you. So we say, have mercy on them O Lord, and also on all who have been their victims.

We pray for all in the security forces and for their families who worry for their safety. Help them to remain even-handed and just even to people who hate them, and save them from the corrupting force of power. We pray for those in prison and for their relatives. We pray for prison officers. Help them to carry out their duties with firmness yet with some under-standing of, and feeling for, the prisoners they guard. We pray for judges and magistrates and their families. Bless the work of our courts, and grant that true justice may be done, and may be seen to be done. We pray for all our politicians. Help them to find new ways to lead us forward out of all the sterile conflicts which for so long have disturbed our peace. Be with all our churches and their leaders. Prepare our hearts this Advent and Christmas to receive anew our Lord in all his weakness and humility, and may he be for all of us in a new way the Prince of Peace.

On another occasion the service of prayer and reconciliation was again held on Advent Sunday (23 November 1997). In this case Ken officiated and Gerry led in prayer. The pulpit was shared by the Rt Rev John Dunlop, Moderator of the Presbyterian Church in Ireland and Dr Sean Brady, the new Catholic Archbishop of Armagh, successor to Cahal Daly. Both of them spoke on the theme, 'How does Jesus Christ want our churches to relate to each other?'

The Universal Week of Prayer for Christian Unity allows for an annual service sponsored by the Clonard-Fitzroy Fellowship. One recent service, held at Clonard's Church of the Most Holy Redeemer on 17 January 1999, stands out in the memory of those I interviewed, because of the poignancy of Gerry's homily.

> Why have we invited Ken Newell and the members of Fitzroy Presbyterian Church to be with us at this Eucharist? So that we can reflect more fruitfully on the mystery of the Eucharist and the church – the one bread and the one body; that is, to do theology together. Doing theology together has been a marvellous adventure for us as disciples of Jesus from Fitzroy and from Clonard.
>
> The adventure of doing theology together is not in having arguments with one another. The fruitless days of soul-destroying arguments about doctrine are gone where Clonard and Fitzroy are concerned. We do theology by befriending one another and sharing the story of our faith – our experience of Jesus walking with us on the road of life. That is the way of doing theology which Bishop Jeremy Taylor, Anglican Bishop of Dromore, recommended in a lecture in Trinity College Dublin in the 1660s: 'Theology is rather a divine life than a divine knowledge. In heaven, indeed, we shall first see and then love, but here on earth we must first love, and love will open our eyes as well as our hearts, and we shall see, and then perceive and understand.'
>
> Doing theology in this way has shown us that Ken and the members of Fitzroy are Presbyterian members of the church for us, not against us. And members of Fitzroy have come to know that we are Catholics for them, not against them. Indeed, we are all disciples of Jesus, not against one another but for one another, so that together we can be his

witnesses before the whole world.

Doing theology this way led Ken to say 'yes' to me when I invited him to be with me in the sanctuary of the church at Bernard Kane's funeral mass. We will never forget that day, nor will Bernard's Presbyterian relatives who were there. Doing theology this way led me to say 'yes' to Ken when he invited me to preach the homily at the baptism of a little girl in Fitzroy Church. The girl's mother was Presbyterian, her father was Catholic. The Catholic granny stayed away because she then believed that the baptism at Fitzroy was not a Catholic baptism. During the homily I saw the tears rolling down the cheeks of the Presbyterian granny from Co Armagh. At the end of the service, she came up and embraced me.

Doing theology in this way will lead us in God's time to share fully in the one Eucharist. The norms of the bishop's recent letter, *One Bread, One Body*, do not permit us to share fully in the Eucharist today with the disciples of Jesus from Fitzroy. We are really one church with them; we are not yet fully one church with them. Our communion is real because it is rooted in the heart of God our Father. The Word made flesh has made us one. Our communion is imperfect, partial, and incomplete because it is not yet fully visible. Our communion is a child which is growing to be an adult. Neither of us will be adult churches until we have grown to be fully one church. When will that day come? Let us continue doing theology together, praying together and doing all we can. That day may be the Sunday of the first Universal Week of Prayer for Christian Unity in the new millennium, that is, next year. Everything is possible. God must be allowed to surprise us.

Having seen all the above regarding the people and the programmes of the Clonard-Fitzroy Fellowship, a question arises: how effective was the Fellowship's work, and how did its goals get translated into reality? In this regard, a major sign of the Fellowship's coming of age was an opportunity for a self study, funded by a small grant which Gerry Reynolds had secured from the Ireland Fund. With that money the Clonard-Fitzroy Fellowship engaged a consultant, Dr Johnston McMaster, himself a Methodist minister and a member of the academic staff at the Irish School of Ecumenics in Dublin. The McMaster study was done in May 1998, and when published, it was given a title, *With Renewed Intent: An Evaluation and Strategic Plan, Clonard-Fitzroy Fellowship*, and ran to thirty typescript pages. While we can only highlight a few items from the McMaster report, it is an excellent source for us to assess the work of the Fellowship on the eve of its receiving the Pax Christi Peace Prize in 1999. We should mention that for a good part of the 1990s, the Fellowship was chaired and led by Chris Williamson, whose leadership and dependability was extremely valuable throughout, and especially so at the time of the McMaster study.

When the leadership of the Clonard-Fitzroy Fellowship, clergy and lay, met with Johnston McMaster it was decided that his report should have two parts, one retrospective and the second prospective; that is, the first part should evaluate what had been accomplished and the second to make a strategic plan. At the heart of the whole process were three interactive workshops, the average attendance at which was about forty people. The three meetings were each about two and one-half hours long.

The report *With Renewed Intent* is written in bureaucratic language that characterises a management style of interest in a group's structure and function in relation to stated goals and desired outcomes. At the same time, the consultant was well-attuned to the obvious fact that this particular group had a religious origin and purpose. The first questions were about group identity, e.g., who are we and what are we here for? The three sets of workshop participants came up with differing points of emphasis. The first group gave a theological answer: 'We are a group of Christians from Fitzroy and Clonard congregations who, being disturbed by the brokenness of God's people in Northern Ireland, and urged on by our common love of the Lord Jesus, came together in all our diversity to fulfill his will for his church under the guidance of the Holy Spirit.' The second group offered a functional analysis: 'We are a group of fellow Christians in Ireland who are taking seriously Christ's prayer that we should be one. We are a sign of unity within a divided church. We are a sign of hope and friendship in a hurting community.' The third group reflected on the group's identity in terms of aspirations: 'We are Christians from Protestant and Catholic traditions. We want to know more about each other's denomination. We want to be with each other to show that we are all not angry stereotypes. We want to show that we can live with our next door neighbours whoever they are. We want to explore Christian issues on a spiritual level.'

The three ways of identifying the Clonard-Fitzroy fellowship were thought to be valuable, even though emphasising different angles of vision. All three realised that identities proceeded from actions engaged in together, and the constant need to bring idealised formulations into practical realities. After seventeen years in existence, most of the Fellowship's members were aware of how much had been accomplished: the sense of comfort with each other; the success of crossing religious and class boundaries; the deepening of faith when it is shared with others not from one's own tradition; the sense of awareness about being alert to discriminatory language and behaviour.

McMaster then led the Fellowship people into a discussion in which the members would 'own' the weaknesses of the group. One agreed-to weakness that emerged was a culture of politeness, in which group identity was protected, either by not raising tough issues or by coming too quickly to agreement on them. It was admitted that, perhaps, being polite really masked lack of confidence in the group's ability to sustain substantive and substantial disagreement. Further, another weakness was 'owned': because the Fellowship was a voluntary organisation with no staff, it suffered the fate of all such groups, such as organisational informality and unclear lines of communication. Further, the McMaster report touched a sensitive nerve when it said: 'The group may well experience tension on this issue because of the social differences between Clonard and Fitzroy. That a considerable social gap is transcended by a shared sense of Christian identity is positive, but it does not overcome the reality of seeing though different lenses and of having different needs and expectations.' Another weakness noted was that the majority of those participating had been from the Clonard side. The report observed that the continued health of the Clonard-Fitzroy Fellowship must require an increase in the number of Fitzroy participants. The report was hopeful that this could be accomplished, especially since the Fellowship had a long enough existence to share a significant story of commonly 'owned' events.

Finally, the strategic plan provided an interesting possible roadmap, but some members of the Fellowship told me that it was going to be difficult to implement. The plan drew from the hopes and aspirations of the people involved, but its goals looked hard to achieve. One of the hopes articulated in the plan was that there had to be more, and new, members for the work of the Fellowship to be maintained, much less grow. But, the fact of life at Fitzroy Church was that there were many competing activities, which would make it difficult to expand the member-ship of those committed to the reconciling and ecumenical voc-ation of the Fellowship. For reasons noted, but not fully explored, there were more consistent members of the Fellowship from the Clonard side and a disproportionate amount of leadership from the Fitzroy side. This was going to have to change if the next level of activity was to be attained. At the time of this writing, the Fellowship was continuing to be a successful small group, but the questions about membership and its balance between the two churches were still being discussed.

The other major recommendation in the strategic plan that all agreed would be desirable – a person to take the lead in admin-istration – has also proven elusive. Organisational informality was recognised as vital if programming spontaneity was to be continued. At the same time, too much spontaneity led to incon-sistency in terms of the overall pursuit of the Fellowship's mis-sion. The report suggested that Clonard and Fitzroy might be able to find a retired person to take the administrator post if the preferred recommendation, a paid position, could not be funded.

Some of the people I interviewed acknowledged that an administrator would solve problems of inconsistency and lack of communication, but they were a bit wary about it too, as though a process of institutionalisation might rob the Fellowship of its great quality of 'people-to-people' that had made the friendships so satisfying. Once again, at the time of this writing, five years after the McMaster report, no decision had been made on the question of an administrator. Yet, even though parts of the strategic plan have not been enacted, and some members wondered about the value received for the money spent, most of the members of the Clonard-Fitzroy Fellowship, and its sustaining churches, were glad to have had the opportunity to work with Johnston McMaster and to have the chance to review their work so thoroughly.

In the next year, 1999, there was another organisation that was reviewing the work of the Clonard-Fitzroy Fellowship. Pax Christi is the peace movement within the Catholic Church. It was founded after the Second World War to promote peace and reconciliation between the German and the French peoples. In time, it was to become a fully international peace movement that, even though connected to the Catholic Church, is highly respected by all for its consistent advocacy of 'the peace of Christ', as its name suggests. Each year it gives a peace prize that recognises people or groups who are working for peace and reconciliation at the grassroots level. Some people refer to it as a religious equivalent of the Nobel Peace Prize. In prior years, those receiving the prize had worked in various ways in, for example, Angola, Brazil, East Timor, the former Czechoslovakia and the former Yugoslavia. The recipients had never been from Ireland and had always been from the Roman Catholic tradition. In 1999, that was to change in both respects: the award was given to an Irish group, the Clonard-Fitzroy Fellowship; and in the person of Ken Newell, who accepted the award along with Gerry Reynolds on behalf of the Fellowship, the first time to a Protestant.

On 30 November 1999 many people from the Fitzroy Church

and the Church of the Most Holy Redeemer drove down from Belfast to the Gresham Hotel in Dublin for the awards ceremony. It was significant that it was in Dublin, not Belfast. Pax Christi has a section in most nations, and the Irish section is headquartered in Dublin. It was not lost on those participating that recipients for peace work in Northern Ireland, legally and constitutionally a part of the United Kingdom, went to the capital of another nation to receive their award. At the festive event, people well known in church and state mingled with those known only to the family and friends of the award recipients. The opening prayer set the tone for the evening:

Prayer for a New Society
All nourishing God, your children cry for help
Against the violence of our world:
Where children starve for bread and feed on weapons;
Starve for vision and feed on drugs;
Starve for love and feed on videos;
Starve for peace and die murdered in our streets.

Liberating God, release us from the demons of violence.
Free us today from the disguised demon of deterrence
That puts guns by our pillows and missiles in our skies ...

Abiding God, stretch our sense of family to include our
    neighbours.
Stretch our sense of neighbour to include our enemies
Until our response to you finally respects and embraces
All creation as precious sacraments of your presence.

Fr Gerry Reynolds and Rev Ken Newell were extraordinarily honoured to have the introduction of recipients be given by Mairéad Corrigan Maguire, herself a recipient of the Nobel Peace Prize in 1977:

It is my pleasure to introduce the recipients of the Pax Christi International Peace Prize – the Clonard-Fitzroy Fellowship. On behalf of all gathered here, I welcome Rev Ken Newell and Fr Gerry Reynolds, and members of the Fellowship who travelled from Belfast to be here in Dublin on this wonderful occasion.

We applaud the tremendous courage shown by Rev

Newell and Fr Reynolds in the early years of the Fellowship
when they took the brave step of crossing the political and religious divide and coming together as ministers of God to
study scripture and work with members of their respective
churches. In a society as tragically divided as Northern
Ireland, this was indeed an inspired act of faith in God, in
themselves and in each other. It took courage also for the lay
members of both communities to break out of the security
and coziness of familiar surroundings and begin to share and
learn from others of a different tradition. We thank them for
their faithful commitment to friendship and practical peacemaking. Their lives and work as laity in prayer and action is
most important. They show us that it is important to pray but
we must also act. Our actions too are not only on an individual level, but we must also work to change structures and institutions which are unjust.

This work has ranged from the deeply spiritual to the
deeply political, as all genuine work for equality, human
rights and non-violence must do. The deep friendship between Rev Newell and Fr Reynolds, and the Fellowship
members, has enabled them to cross over boundaries traditionally closed to each other. As Rev Newell explained to me,
'Gerry and I took each other to places where we could not get
to before.'

I would like to thank the members of the Fellowship for
their faithfulness for so many years. Sometimes what we do
seems small and unimportant. Your work as a group of
friends is important for peace in Northern Ireland. We know
that, when the Good Friday Agreement is fully implemented,
the people on the ground have to take ownership of it and
build peace together. We must make Northern Ireland work
and become 'best friends'. This can only be done in exactly
the way you are doing it. To build a culture of peace and non-
violence is the work of the people and the churches. It is a
challenge, a joy, but also a lot of hard work. Thank you for
your example, you give us all hope. Blessed are the peacemakers of the Fitzroy-Clonard Fellowship.

The recipients were further honoured by the presence of
Michael Sabbah, Patriarch of the Latin Rite, who came from
Jerusalem to make the award for Pax Christi. He said he was the

one honoured by taking part in these festivities, and on behalf of Pax Christi, 'We are delighted that the 1999 Peace Prize is going to the Fitzroy-Clonard Fellowship. Their work in building the kingdom of the Prince of Peace in the traumatised community of Northern Ireland has been a shining example and a beacon of hope.'

The highlight of the speeches was the acceptance speech given by Gerry, on behalf of Ken and all the people of the two churches:

> I stand in awe at the fact that the simple friendship which developed since the early 1980s between Presbyterians of Fitzroy congregation and Catholics associated with us, and the ordinary things we have done together should today, at this gathering, be recognised by Pax Christi as 'exemplary work towards building the kingdom of the Prince of Peace'. I accept the award not just on behalf of those more immediately involved in the developing relationship between Clonard and Fitzroy. I accept it on behalf of all those associated with us who have striven over the years at the grassroots to develop the dialogue of faith and the search for reconciliation and peace in Ireland.
>
> I think that the Clonard-Fitzroy Fellowship is primarily about witnessing to a different God in our divided sectarian society. Not a God who divides but who unites us through Jesus Christ, and his Spirit of Love, for the task of transforming our history. We witness to a God who is with us in every human face and in every place where people gather to worship him. A God of kindness and faithful love. A God who sets no bounds to his love and compels us to set none to ours. A God of life and of the ritual that illumines life. A God who delights in unity and diversity.
>
> In the Clonard-Fitzroy Fellowship we are learning that a united church makes visible that a higher power is at work in our divided society, and that the world is different because of the death and resurrection of Jesus. A divided church appears the same as other human organisations. We need to become explorers like Abraham. For the Catholic congregations the promised land is among their Protestant brothers and sisters; for the Protestant congregations it is among their Catholic brothers and sisters. As we prepare for Jubilee 2000

we believe that we are being called to cast off the sectarian religion we have inherited to become a 'community of friends'.
We are not to blame for what we have inherited. Those who
passed on the 'fractured tradition' to us are not to blame –
they acted in good faith. But we have no excuse if we pass on a
divided church to the first generation of the new millennium.

If you were to ask me 'What has been Ken's impact on my
life and mine on his?' I would give this simple answer: 'We
help one another to walk with God.' At the first meeting in
Clonard monastery between a group of Sinn Féin leaders and
some Protestant clergy to search for peace together and for a
democratic way forward out of our 'Troubles,' Ken was the
one who invited me to open with a prayer. I chose Psalm 85:
'I will hear what the Lord God has to say, a voice that speaks
of peace.' At an angry meeting with UDP members in
September 1994, in between the IRA and Loyalist ceasefires
and two months after the IRA had killed their leader Ray
Smallwood, Ken's initiative in setting up a moment of prayer
put our discussions in the new perspective of God's presence
with us in all the pain, anger and confusion. Building the
kingdom of the Prince of Peace at grassroots level is a long
difficult haul that is not for the faint-hearted.

The evening ended with a concert presented by a joint choir
of the two churches. As well as the sort of religious music one
might expect at such an occasion, there were several informal
musical numbers presented that showed the affection the two
congregations have for the two clergy. One was sung to the tune
of 'Molly Malone,' and was full of fun poked at the two comrades, part of which invoked a changed world in which one
might see 'Moderator Gerry and Cardinal Ken'. It was a warm
and hilarious conclusion to a memorable evening.

In the afterglow of that lovely evening in Dublin, I asked
some members of the Fellowship where they might go from
there. In the first place they all needed some time to let the
award sink in, and to recognise how far they had come together
in these years. Most of the Fellowship members I interviewed
joined Gerry in being 'awed' by the international recognition of
'their wee group'. Because of the publicity associated with the

Pax Christi Prize, their Fellowship became well known in all parts of Ireland. When asked about it, most seemed quite deeply affected by the memory – filtered back through the Pax Christi award evening – that they had done something of worth in their lives; in the context of the Troubles, they had made a difference. I asked a number of people how they saw the future, and if they could see the continued success of the Clonard-Fitzroy Fellowship beyond the leadership span of Gerry Reynolds and Ken Newell. Understandably, hardly anyone wanted to contemplate life at either Clonard or Fitzroy without the two leaders. All those interviewed reaffirmed that without the leadership of Ken and Gerry, the two churches and most of the people would not have gone on this exhilarating journey of friendship and faith. Further, most respondents thought that their church officers were by now so committed to the journey of faith together that any replacements for Reynolds and Newell at Clonard and Fitzroy would have to be equally committed to that vision. The newly emerging leadership demonstrates the deep consensus of the commitment to the joint vision. For example, at Newell's suggestion, the Fellowship has been chaired since 1999 by a Fitzroy member, Roel Dekker, whose quiet demeanor and steady leadership have been much appreciated by all. So while the future was, of course, unclear, the result of my raising the questions about continuity and viability left most respondents quietly confident that their two churches could, and would, sustain what they had begun two decades earlier.

CHAPTER FOUR

Other Religious Works of Gerry Reynolds and Ken Newell

The Clonard-Fitzroy Fellowship was the main thrust of the friendship between Ken and Gerry. But it was by no means the only things they did. While the Fellowship's great success spurred on other people to accomplish many things, Ken and Gerry encouraged each other in different areas. They worked together, independently, and with others, in many ventures beyond the specific work of the Clonard-Fitzroy Fellowship. In this chapter we will illumine those other religious activities in which Gerry and Ken participated that would further their vocation to pursue mutual understanding and reconciliation. In the next chapter we will focus on their activities that had direct bearing on political reconciliation.

To introduce this subject it may help us to think about the chemistry between the two men, and the qualities each brought to each other in this special friendship. Then, we will characterise the leadership styles of Reynolds and Newell as it bears on our hope to understand them. In Protestant Northern Irish speech, a great compliment is paid to a person who is referred to as 'down-to-earth'. Some observers of Northern Irish (and Northern English and Scottish) life extol the virtues of earthiness, as compared to the southern English, who are often perceived as having views of themselves that mirror their elevated – some would say pretentious – accents. Especially among Ulster-Scot Presbyterians, even though they want their clergy well trained and good preachers, they relate very much to a practical, earthy (though surely never vulgar) style. Ken Newell would see himself, and be seen by his people, in precisely that mold. By contrast to the self-understanding of Ulster-Scot culture, Irish Catholic culture puts great value on poetry, song and on – especially for their obviously unmarried clergy – an other-worldliness characterised by deep intellectuality and spirituality. Gerry Reynolds is much revered for being the intellectual and visionary. In my own observation of the two friends, I am sure that there is something in that rough characterisation. They and their people joke, though with serious intent, that Ken is the practical get-the-job-done partner, while I heard Gerry charac-terised by both laity and his own fellow clergy at the monastery as a 'dreamer' who has his feet planted firmly in the clouds (as Sandra Rutherford's birthday song recorded). Yet, for all the wordplay about it, I think that laity and clergy alike believe this to be a great combination, in which Ken and Gerry, and the members of their churches who follow them, trade off the rela-tive gifts of the other. In time though, the qualities of one begin to rub off on the other, with Ken showing visionary qualities and Gerry practical ones. But Gerry sees the vision of what the churches and cultures of Ireland might be like through the works of grace; Ken sees the vision too but he has been more ori-ented to trying new experiments in the empowerment of people. Whatever the chemistry between them, many people have bene-fited by this extraordinary yet unlikely pair of friends.

In the next pages we will observe Reynolds and Newell on their journeys of faith, and see where it has taken them. While we will emphasise many aspects other than the Clonard-Fitzroy Fellowship, that was always the baseline from which Gerry and Ken moved out, either together or encouraging each other in making common cause with others.

In trying to describe the various other 'religious' activities engaged in by Rev Ken Newell and Fr Gerry Reynolds, we are faced with a problem of how to proceed. All their activities and patterns of engagement were, in their minds, related to every-thing else they did. So, for example, the choice for Gerry and Ken to attend funerals of victims of sectarian violence was not a whole other category of behaviour, but part of their overall voc-ation of reconciliation in church and society. Further, their work

with the Clonard-Fitzroy Fellowship (our last chapter) was not
at all sealed off from their political work (our next chapter). But
since we delineate different strands of their work for analytical
purposes, it is well that we acknowledge our partial distortion of
the 'real world' in which Gerry and Ken live.

We have already noted in several places above that a main
strategy was fairly straightforward and simple, that people and
groups could only be reconciled when they got to know each
other; therefore, human contact and expressions of solidarity
were the first things to be organised. We have already seen that
when Fr Christy, later Gerry, brought people together around
the Bible, good things happened, religiously and politically. The
main strategy, then, was to create venues in which it was natural
for people in both communities to meet and to have direct
experience of the goodwill and human empathy of a person
from the 'other side'.

The tragic circumstances of the Troubles in the 1970s and
1980s produced unwelcome but useful occasions for cross-community contact. Let us recall that a large majority of the people
killed in the Troubles died in the first fifteen years after 1969. By
the mid-1980s, many people in Northern Ireland were sick of the
violence and weary from the shock of what one journalist called
'the latest atrocity'. It occurred to Ken, Gerry and Sam Burch
that, as clergy, they were in a kind of privileged position, in that
it was not unnatural for them to minister to, and console, families of those killed in sectarian violence, even if not members of
their own congregations. They determined to start going to the
funerals of the victims, or going to the homes at the time of the
wake. Of course, they phoned ahead to see if their presence
would be welcomed and that they would not disrupt the event.
Mostly their offers were warmly welcomed and their ministry
much appreciated. Sometimes Ken and Gerry went together
(though Gerry often worked with Sam Burch in these efforts),
most often with other ecumenical clergy. Sometimes the occasions called for Protestants or Catholics only (each to visit the
opposite community), depending on the sensitivity of the situ-

ation. While the procedures may have varied, the impact of these visits did not: they were widely acclaimed as excellent gestures of Christian grace, and of what the future must look like if the people of Northern Ireland were ever to extricate themselves from the painful and frustrating world of the Troubles. The various newspapers in the Belfast area thought these visits worthy of enough note to give them prominent placement in their pages.

On 16 November 1982 Mr Patrick Murphy was at his place of business, a greengrocery on Mount Merrion Avenue, in the Rosetta district of Belfast, an area known to be 'mixed' between Protestants and Catholics. Although he had no known association with paramilitary activity, and was a church-oriented family man, he was murdered in cold blood at the counter in his shop by an unknown Loyalist gunman. His daughters, Collete and Claire, were in the back of the shop when they heard the shooting, and it was they who came first to the body. His wife, Barbara, and four other children would be told the news later.

The surviving Murphys were joined at the funeral by an estimated one thousand people from the area. Friends and relatives guessed that about equal numbers of Catholics and Protestants crowded into St Bernadette's Church for the funeral Mass. Among the mourners that day were forty Protestant clergy. Those in the group came to pay their respects and to protest the sectarian murder of an innocent man. There were representatives from the three main Protestant denominations: Church of Ireland, Methodist and Presbyterians (including four former moderators of the PCI: Alfred Martin, Austin Fulton, J. H. R. Gibson and John Davey).

Ken Newell had organised this extraordinary display of sympathy and solidarity along with clerical activists in the Methodist Church, the Church of Ireland and some of the smaller evangelical churches, but it was to Ken that the media people went for comment. He said that 'We wish to let it be known that the Protestant people are deeply concerned and feel for the Catholics who have suffered at the hands of Protestant gunmen.' He added that Protestant clergy would be visiting the Murphys and other families in the Belfast area bereaved by sectarian murders. He also hoped that his Protestant clergy colleagues would join him in attending other funeral Masses, as need arose and their schedules permitted. Ken went further. In respect of Catholic clergy, he acknowledged that many were already engaged on an individual basis in the work of consoling the bereaved. But he hoped they would become more public about it, and as a group share in the pain and grief of the families of innocent Protestant victims and of the security forces. Ken observed that he and other Protestant clergy had a special role to play in areas where Catholics felt under particular threat; by the same token, he encouraged Catholic clergy to seize the opportunity to minister to Protestants in places like south Armagh and Co Fermanagh, where minority Protestants felt under enormous threat.

To another newspaper Ken acknowledged his down-to-earth style of practical leadership. He said that he organised the clergy presence by phoning around to other sympathetic clergy who 'want to show our abhorrence of violence from whatever quarter. By going to these funerals we plan to demonstrate that there are people who are supremely dedicated to Christ and who have deep love in their hearts for their fellow countrymen, Protestant and Catholic. … We want to show that some people still have the ability to scream out at murder: "This is so awful that it has to stop".'

Ken and the other Protestant clergy were commended for the courageous display of solidarity in an editorial in the *Belfast Telegraph*. He also received many letters of support from individuals in both Northern Ireland and in the Republic of Ireland. But, along with the laudatory comments, there were some interesting points of analysis in the press. In an editorial in the *Irish News* on the day of Patrick Murphy's funeral in 1982, praise for the presence of the Protestant clergy was joined to some concerns that asked uncomfortable questions:

We trust we shall not be misunderstood if we point out that implicit in their call is the dreadful recognition that these tragedies will continue. ... As Christians we owe more to the victims of violence than to stand in unison beside their relatives at the graveside. We may be accused of being harsh in the present suffering of so many if we add that it is not virtuous to be naïve. Surely it is relevant to say that we are being most perfectly Christian and human when we exercise our intellect searchingly on the root causes of the violence in our midst.

Ken Newell would agree with the editorial writer that much work needed to be done in rooting out sectarian violence. But he would also insist that the desperate situation required remedial measures, the first steps on a long journey. One of Patrick Murphy's neighbours on Mount Merrion Avenue wrote to Ken to thank him for the Protestant clergy presence in her church, adding that she hoped her own Catholic clergy would do the same for Protestant victims' families. Ken received other communications too. About a week later, he received a letter from a person highly placed in the Presbyterian Church, which letter gave with one hand and took with the other: it praised Ken for organising the Protestant presence at the funeral Mass; but it noted that phoning around in an *ad hoc* manner 'put people on the spot'. The writer was obviously reflecting the private opposition to Ken's initiative that some Presbyterian clergy had expressed but would not say so publicly. He even suggested that Ken ask only the openly willing to participate. One can see why Ken was often dismayed at such tepid support; he often wondered to himself how ministers or priests could sit in their Manses and Rectories when people from their local communities have been killed, and not go and visit their homes or attend their funerals because they belong 'to the other side' or 'lived outside the boundaries of their parish or presbytery'. Sometimes 'theological differences' were presented as the reason not to participate. But this always sounded to Ken like an excuse. He thought, 'It must be something deeper – like fear, or emotional apartheid. If murder doesn't get you away from your study, what can? How can you preach about the crucifixion of Jesus in Jerusalem 2000 years ago and switch off emotionally from the crucifixion of ordinary people who live half a mile away?' One can see why he drew strength from Cecil Kerr and the people of the Renewal Movement.

It was the encouragement of Catholics that really told Ken he was on the right track. A letter from a nun who lived in the Republic disclosed that Ken's example of solidarity had fired her determination to try to start an interdenominational prayer group in her town. She went around to the clergy of all the major denominations to ask their support. While she was received graciously by all, when the meeting time came, no one from either the Church of Ireland or the Presbyterian Church turned up. But the meeting nevertheless went on with about equal numbers of Catholics and Methodists. Ken was grateful for the good work spreading across Ireland, but one could also wonder what some Protestants in that community were thinking.

Keeping a bit longer with the point of visiting the bereaved and of expressing solidarity 'across the divide', the letter that encouraged Ken most of all was from Peter Bates, a Catholic man from Dublin. He had read about the courage of Ken and the other Protestant clergy and, in response, Bates decided to contribute in his own way. He believed it was his vocation to write letters of condolence to the families of all victims of the Troubles in the North. Ken wrote back and gave Peter Bates some practical advice about how to proceed. The latter then began a career of letter writing that lasted seven years, from 1984 to 1991, when personal circumstances required that he stop. Peter himself received many moving replies in response to his letters, in which people expressed great gratitude for the support and prayers that families – especially Protestants – believed they had received. Through a personal connection at work, Peter was asked to give the communion meditation at a Mass in the parish church in Malahide, Dublin. In attendance that day was Sister Teresa, prioress of the nearby Carmelite Community. She too was moved by Peter's testimony, and the evocation of the example of Ken Newell prompted her to invite Ken to preach on the feast of St Columba, 1996. We have discussed that in the previous chapter because the visit to Malahide had included members of the Clonard-Fitzroy Fellowship. Once again, we see the connection between the various initiatives begun by Ken and Gerry.

The final example to be offered about visiting the bereaved – or, as Ken and Gerry would say, of incarnating the gospel – will take a few pages to tell. But it is worthwhile to allot some space to it because this story gets close to the heart of the problem of forgiveness we are thinking about. Ken wrote his annual letter to the Fitzroy congregation in February 1979. He had previously thought of writing about theologically-interesting but sociologically 'nice' subjects. But the revelations of the atrocities by the so-called 'Shankill Butchers' had changed his mind. (These men got their name because they had stolen implements from a butcher shop, which they then used on their victims.) Ken was convinced that Fitzroy Church needed to face up to, and react to, the brutal killings of innocent Catholic civilians who happened to be picked out by these Protestant, Loyalist criminals. Ken wrote that if his church people wanted only 'nice' religion then they should not read the rest of his letter. The disturbing material to follow, he wrote, was surely not nice, but it was the reality in their city, on which Christians must shine the light of the gospel. It was very challenging for Fitzroy folk to read the following: 'Religion that will not face up to the realities brought to the surface by the "Shankill Butchers" is only a narcotic, an opiate for the people. It is a false religion and its prophets are false.'

Eleven men of the murder squad were on trial as Ken was writing in the winter of 1979. All were to be convicted of their crimes and were to serve long jail sentences. The leaders were named Lenny Murphy, Billy Moore and Bobby Bates. The *Belfast Telegraph* reporter, Deric Henderson, wrote (20 February 1979), that 'they killed savagely, without mercy or pity. They killed innocent people because they were the "wrong" religion.' Henderson noted that even the detectives – Jimmy Nesbitt and

Jackie Fitzsimmons – themselves toughened by years of investigating similar grizzly scenes, were unprepared for what they found in the cases against Murphy, Moore and Bates.

It seems that on the night of 3 February 1977, Joe Morrissey, a 52-year-old Catholic man, was walking home after some hours in a pub with friends. Two of the 'Butchers' were waiting in a car outside St Patrick's Church with murder on their minds. As Morrissey passed the church, the two accosted him and he tried to resist them on St Patrick's steps. The two thugs dragged him into a car, in which he was clubbed on the head with a hatchet. Further down the road the attackers stopped and dragged Morrissey out of the car. Billy Moore then produced a long, sharp butcher knife, and pulled it along the victim's throat, an act that surely took his life. But that was not enough for the supposed defenders of Protestant, Loyalist Ulster. One of them retrieved the hatchet and repeatedly bludgeoned Morrissey's head and lifeless upper body. The coroner's report noted some 27 wounds inflicted. Ken's letter quoted the judge in the trial: 'The Butcher gang killings are a lasting monument to blind bigotry.'

Some of Newell's parishioners understandably winced when reading such material in a pastoral letter. But Ken pushed them even further by insisting that this sort of physical violence grew out of a culture in which bigotry and hatred had almost become normal. He insisted that Christians must both acknowledge this fact and then bring healing where they can.

> There are many people who would never lift a gun or plant a bomb, yet if you listen to the way they speak and observe their attitudes, it is obvious just how strong is their hostility and bitterness. Mental and emotional violence within a person towards other persons who differ religiously or politically is another way of describing 'hate', and the Bible is clear that we cannot share the life of God and hate those whom we should love.

Ken concluded his letter with a ringing call for Fitzroy Church to rally behind a church-wide vocation for peace and justice, both inter-personally and in society.

The Shankill Butchers, as said, received long prison sentences for their crimes. The judge clearly intended that they never be released from prison but, in the case of Bobby Bates, he was released after nineteen years. We are discussing this case here because of a controversy involving Gerry Reynolds some twenty years after the murders described. It involved Bobby Bates, nicknamed 'Basher' Bates, because his personal signature in the murders to which the gang confessed was to bash in the faces of the victims. In the person of Basher Bates, one has the distinct impression of engaging as nearly a pure form of evil as one is likely to find. Therefore, it is particularly striking to learn that in prison Bobby Bates turned his life around, became a born-again Christian, and was thereafter determined to make such amends as were possible. The news of Bates' conversion was seen by some as a bit facile, stretching credulity and possibly a tactic to get out of jail. Especially for some Catholics in west Belfast, this was bitter medicine to be asked to swallow.

When Bates was released from prison in 1996, he expressed his determination to behave differently and he was an apparent model citizen in encouraging others to behave peacefully. But his presence in society as a free man was apparently too difficult for an unknown person to bear. On 11 June 1997 Bobby Bates was shot dead outside a drop-in centre on the Shankill Road where he had been working. The funeral was attended by more than a thousand people, but there were no paramilitary trappings. The chaplain who knew Bobby in prison spoke of the genuine conversion he had experienced there: 'His was not a conversion of convenience.' The service was graced by the presence of Mairéad Corrigan Maguire, who spoke to the same point: Bates 'had repented, asked forgiveness and showed remorse for what he had done. Like all of us, Bobby Bates was in need of God's mercy. He took the lives of many people and we must never forget the pain and loss their relatives will carry with them for ever. But Bobby Bates was also a victim.'

The Peace People also organised a memorial service at the

spot where Bobby Bates has been shot. Fr Gerry Reynolds spoke at that service in memorable terms: 'I wanted to come and be a witness to the power of God to transform people; a power that transformed Bobby Bates and it can transform every single person and group in our society.' Some people in the Clonard area of the Falls Road, while they have every respect for Gerry, found it very difficult to follow their beloved priest in this case. One of them, a relative of a Bates murder victim, said, 'As far as Bates is concerned, I have very little sympathy for him, if any. I don't know how anybody who could call themselves a Christian could attach themselves to the atrocities he carried out.' But another person could forgive. A relative of Joe Morrissey, whose murder was described above, had written to the Bates family to tell of his sympathy for them. Bates' sister, Margaret Holland, publicly thanked the Morrissey family, saying how much it meant to her family to receive their sympathy. In fact, Margaret Holland had met Fr Gerry by chance while walking up on the Glencairn Hill above the Shankill. She remembered, 'He was just up for his walk and he started to talk to me. He didn't know who I was. We were just sharing the love of God. Then I told him about the way the Lord had changed my brother's life.' The newspaper, the *Belfast Newsletter*, carried a picture in its 13 June 1997 edition of Fr Gerry shaking hands with Margaret Holland, as he brought condolences to the family.

It was a test then – and continues for us who hear about it now – to accept that this surely evil person had been forgiven his crimes. Some people on the Falls Road also agree that being asked to forgive Basher Bates came hard on their hearts and minds. But as Gerry would insist, here we have the essence of the mysterious power of the gospel. In their own strength and will, the families of those horrendously murdered by the likes of Bobby Bates might not find the grace to forgive. But in and through the power of the cross, sufficient grace can be found. If the gospel of Jesus cannot handle the case of Bobby Bates, then the whole Christian story is in question.

We now move to further activities of Gerry and Ken which

we lump under the heading 'religious', although recalling our previous point about how all their activities were of a piece. After the meeting at Fitzroy Church in 1986, when the Clonard-Fitzroy Fellowship – with the full and expressed approval of the Fitzroy Kirk Session – made religious history by having a current Moderator of the PCI and a Catholic bishop preach together from the same pulpit, Ken and Gerry wanted to keep the momentum going. One main concern of both men was to continue to provide venues where Protestants and Catholics could meet in a natural way. They were very concerned about the clergy of their respective denominations who, for the most part, had little personal knowledge of each other and even less contact. They decided to have a one day theological conference at St Clement's, the retreat house on the Antrim Road, north Belfast, which was owned and operated by the Redemptorist order (the same order as in Clonard monastery).

In the first meeting of 'The Catholic-Protestant Theological Conference' series, on 23 January 1987, Ken and Gerry brought a very experienced and credible group of speakers together, on the topic 'Exploring the Mystery of Our Lord Jesus Christ, Mary and the Church.' The leading speaker was a theological heavyweight from the Protestant and Reformed side, Dr James Torrance, Professor of Theology at the University of Aberdeen. His comments were both provocative and irenic: provocative because a traditional Protestant understanding was deconstructed; irenic, because the listeners at St Clement's that day would surely have heard a rendition of what they could share, not what divided them. He remarked that people back in Scotland had asked him how he could go to Belfast and worship with Catholics. To Torrance, that question showed a huge misunderstanding of the Reformation doctrine of grace. He insisted that God does not accept us or reject us on the basis of how we worship or how we formulate the doctrine of grace. Torrance suggested that sectarianism develops when one formulation of grace and of worship says its formulation of the truth is 'the Truth', and then says to others that we will only accept you if you accept our formulations of the truth. In short, if true worship is accepting God's call of grace to participate through the Spirit in communion with the Father, how dare we say that we are not going to worship with others? How dare we impose conditions of acceptance on others when God apparently does not do so? It was the existence of other barriers of human making that continued to divide the churches in Northern Ireland. He called for the examining of those barriers because they can continue to exist if unexamined, but once examined they can not bear the light of scrutiny. He noted that at certain times in the twentieth century, Christians in situations of conflict met to declare their opposition to human-made barriers of exclusion and oppression: in 1934 in Germany there was the Barmen Confession against the world of the Nazis; in 1982 in South Africa there was the Belhar Confession against the world of apartheid. Torrance wondered if it was not the time for a 'Belfast Confession' in which Protestants and Catholics could confess together their exclusive allegiance to Jesus Christ and their mutual desire for a society of peace and justice in Northern Ireland. We do not have the record of the responses to Torrance brought by a Catholic and an Anglican, but some of the approximately one hundred present on the day recall a sense of vitality and purpose this new venue brought to Belfast.

The conferences went on for another ten years, though it is interesting to observe that in the 1990s, the name was changed from 'Catholic-Protestant Conference' to 'Evangelical-Roman Catholic Conference'. This was part of a general trend in the USA and the UK in which a great deal of exchange was going on between the Catholic Church and the theologically conservative end of Protestantism. Also, it was a conscious effort on the part of Ken and Gerry not to allow the good word 'Evangelical' to be the sole preserve of the forces of reaction. By 1995, with cease-fires underway, and many more venues for the two communities to meet having been established in the intervening decade, the topics discussed at the conference would become less theological and more practical and applied. For example, the speakers in 1995 included one Catholic clergy, one Protestant activist, and two political office holders, one from each tradition. In the chair on the day was the then-current Moderator of the Presbyterian Church of Ireland, Dr John Ross, who stated the day's theme, 'building a community in Northern Ireland where all feel valued, a community of firm foundations and effective in its durability.'

Perhaps one reason to explain the change of title for the conferences was Ken Newell's involvement with a movement called Evangelicals and Catholics Together (ETC), a loosely organised association of persons of both Catholic and Protestant origins who had some contact with the Charismatic Renewal. In essence, the Catholics involved had a religious experience that they would describe in Protestant evangelical language. So, the testimony of Catholics ran something like this: 'I was raised in a traditional Catholic home, and did all that was expected of me, and went to church regularly. But I did not have a personal relationship with Jesus. Then an event or set of events brought a crisis in my life that forced me to ask basic questions. Through others I was brought into a Bible study or prayer group, at which I was converted.' The consequent experience of the Holy Spirit was, for some, the sign that God had visited them. They then functionally became 'evangelicals' in that their main goal was to tell the story of their new faith to others so that they too might be converted.

Ken found all of this very encouraging, both, as we have noted above, in terms of the fellowship with the new friends made as well as the purposefulness of those Catholics 'in renewal' wanting to pursue reconciliation with Protestants. But, Ken also saw possibilities within the various Protestant churches to engage Catholics on the basis of the Renewal. So Ken became a person who was known to be sympathetic to the Renewal and especially to Catholics in it. He spoke in several Protestant venues to give some perspective on the Renewal and to try to persuade Protestants to see what was beneficial in it, most notably a new spontaneity in worship and a new awareness that Catholics were – or at least could be – their comrade Christians.

In 1991 he gave talks at both Belfast Bible College and at Union Theological College (of the Presbyterian Church in Ireland). The talks stressed for his Protestant audiences the ways in which the Renewal was good for Protestant churches intrinsically (it would democratise leadership in line with the historic Protestant doctrine of the priesthood of all believers) and instrumentally (it would allow them to be open to co-operative ministry with other believers, especially Catholics, so that reconciliation might be achieved).

A great friend and ally of Ken's was Paddy Monaghan, a leader in evangelical Catholic circles from Dublin. Back in 1983, when Ken organised the side meeting at the PCI General Assembly in Dublin, when Cahal Daly and Alan Flavelle had spoken, it was Paddy who had organised the presence of about fifty Catholic priests and lay people. Of the many things that Ken did along with Monaghan and born-again Catholics, the most public venture was a remarkable little book, *Adventures in Reconciliation* (Eagle Books, 1998), which contained the evangelical-style testimonies of twenty-nine Catholics.

The existence of the book itself was almost more remarkable than its contents. Before a reader ever got to the testimonies, there was a great deal of front end material: a preface, a foreword and five commendations. The five writing commendations were carefully chosen to represent all the points of the religious compass. There were enthusiastic endorsements, along with some fulsome renditions of their own testimonies, by Harold Miller, Church of Ireland Bishop; Trevor Morrow, soon to be Presbyterian Moderator; Ken Wilson, a Methodist Superintendent; Paul Reid, a pastor in one of the new denominations born of the Renewal, The Christian Fellowship Church. The commendation by the new Roman Catholic Archbishop, Seán Brady, was warm, short and correct, but lacking in the testimony-style of the others. The longest single piece in the front matter was the preface by Cardinal Cahal Daly, now succeeded in his episcopal role by Brady. The Cardinal's comments were ambivalent, though he still commended the book. Daly expressed his unease with the unspoken contrast in the book between Christians who were 'born again' and 'Spirit filled' and those Christians who were regular believers but who could claim no conversion experience or special visitation of the Spirit. Daly stated that he could not see a work of the Holy Spirit going on outside the sacraments of the church because, in his view, the Holy Spirit was a gift to the church, not to individuals. For him, this was an important point to make, because if reconciliation between Protestants and Catholics were to go on in church and society, both sides must accept each other as they are in their own self-description, not as they might be if they could describe their religious experiences in the Catholic equivalent of evangelical Protestant terms. Protestants, we might note, had long held that real and true Christians could not be raised in the Catholic Church; and, if they did make a 'decision for Christ', they could not remain in that church (though many Protestants no longer insist on that). Indeed, several of the Protestant clergy commending the book broached that question obliquely, that is, in encouraging Protestant readers of the book to accept these testimonies as the real item and these people as true Christians. For Cardinal Daly, that implication was unacceptable because he believed in the unity of the whole church: 'the unity sought by the worldwide ecumenical movements is a unity between churches and not just between like-minded individuals within churches and independently of those churches.' While Cardinal Daly's contribution was welcomed by, and symbolically important to, the initiators of the book, the dissonance could not but be noted.

In Ken Newell's foreword a more positive chord was sounded. Ken observed that he had never before seen Catholic religious experience commended so openly by Protestant leaders. Moreover, Ken was pleased to say that many of those giving their testimonies were already leaders in their communities in terms of living out the gospel: 'They are confronting the sectarian mindset that still dominates; they are urging the abolition of abusive theological language; they are pressing Christians to involve themselves more convincingly in the peacemaking vocation which is the mark of God's children.'

In another set of dramatically public events in Northern Ireland, the issues of reconciliation and hard-line resistance to change were played out in Limavady through the ministry of David Armstrong. David was the young minister of First Limavady and Magilligan Presbyterian Churches. David and Ken knew each other through the Renewal Movement; they had also been deeply influenced through the work of Canon David Watson of York whose 'Festivals of Faith' throughout Ireland had combined the themes of evangelism, renewal and reconciliation. Back in 1982, there was a new Catholic church being built in Limavady, although there were rumblings of discontent among a certain element of local Protestants. A bomb was set off at the building site by unknown persons. The damage was repaired, the church was completed, and was ready for dedication in early 1985. Armstrong, the Presbyterian minister in Limavady, and very good friend of the Catholic priest, Fr Kevin Mullan, had been personally outraged by the bombing of the Church of Christ the King, as the Catholic church was to be named: 'That foul act struck me at the time as a terrible desecration. The church was dedicated to Christ the King and here were people planting a bomb in the house of the Lord. It was blasphemy – nothing less.' David wanted to attend the dedication, but in view of Protestant disquiet about the new church in town, he felt the need for support among his local Protestant colleagues. He was astonished to find that no support would be forthcoming.

On several occasions David would drop into Fitzroy's Manse in the evening to talk with Ken about the pressures he was under. Ken's admiration for the courage of the young minister in speaking out against the barbarity of blowing up a church was strong, and in crossing the unchallenged religious and sectarian boundaries that run right through the villages, towns and cities of Northern Ireland Ken believed that David was walking in the footsteps of the radical Lord of the gospel. Jesus did it in Galilee and Samaria; David was doing it in Limavady. Ken therefore encouraged him to do what was in his heart to do: accept the invitation to attend the opening of the new Catholic church. In such a simple and Christ-like gesture he would be expressing his best wishes to his Catholic neighbours across the road from First Limavady, challenging hardline attitudes and showing that there is a generous and outgoing side to Presbyterians. Ken told David and the latter quoted it for the newspapers: 'David, you have my love and prayers. You will be doing the right thing.' But, as the *Irish Times* reporter Jane Coyle was to write later, in going to the dedication, David Armstrong 'was signing his professional death warrant'. The opposition to Armstrong's continued ministry in Limavady was led by dissident Presbyterians – The Free Presbyterians – not even in his own parish, but in league with Ian R. K. Paisley. Opposition grew in his own church, and even in the Session. In May of 1985, he had to resign. As Armstrong was about to depart for England, Ken and a group of eighteen other ministers of the Presbyterian Church in Ireland, went public in their support for him, saying in a letter to a newspaper, 'We are making this statement now because Mr Armstrong's vision, personal courage and eventual departure have left a deep impression among many members of the Presbyterian Church in Ireland.' However, knowing he was not alone brought David Armstrong some comfort, but it did not save his ministry for the north of Ireland. He was later received in the Church of England, studied for two years at Oxford, and was ordained an Anglican priest in 1987. He served a church in southern England for four years, and returned to Ireland in September 2000, to serve a Church of Ireland congregation in Co Cork in the Republic. It cost Ken Newell something to support Armstrong in this way. David's departure had a strong emotional impact on Ken; he still recalls the sense of shame he felt that a young, inspiring, courageous and evangelical minister could no longer continue his work in Northern Ireland due to sectarian intimidation. He was a major loss to the ministry of the Presbyterian Church. David appreciated the private and public support he received from a small group of his Presbyterian colleagues, including Ken. David Armstrong, now well-placed in Co Cork, recently looked back on his early career in Limavady, and he reflected on how far he had come out of the fundamentalism that had characterised his early life and ministry. In 2002, he penned a few lines of verse that recall to him the attitudes of conservative evangelicals who harried him out of the Presbyterian Church in Ireland:

Believe as I believe, no more no less
That I am right and no one else, confess
Feel as I feel, think as I think
Eat as I eat and drink as I drink
Look as I look, do as I do
Then and only then will I have fellowship with you.

As well as the many and varied activities of Fr Gerry Reynolds which we will describe herein, one is very interesting and revealing: his resumption of a journalistic career he had earlier in Dublin. What interests us here is his two-year stint as writer of a monthly column for the Belfast newspaper, *The Irish News*. It was called 'Communion', in which Gerry wrote under the pseudonym 'Couturier', signaling once again his love and admiration for Fr Paul Couturier, the man often described as the father of spiritual ecumenism. Gerry Reynolds intended that his column have an ecumenical vision that would encourage his readers to see a future for Christians in Ireland as a journey they would all take together. He began the column in July 1987 and it continued until June 1989, when illness and a year's sabbatical in Jerusalem curtailed 'Couturier's' journalistic career in Belfast. Over the next few pages we will look into some of Gerry's best columns to catch the drift of his thinking and what was in his heart.

The column frequently dealt with challenging and complex matters. But its style was very conversational, allowing ordinary people to believe that they had access to a worthwhile discussion. Further, Gerry encouraged his readers to write in, and he would print parts of their letters and comment on them. In short, the column was both intellectually challenging and folksy, and many people in Belfast still recall 'Communion' with pleasure.

The first column, 7 July 1987, set the tone for what was to come. Reynolds began with a story of a woman friend in Belfast who was taking a theological course that required her to go to her own church on a Sunday as well as the service of another denomination. She had been raised as a Catholic, and at a time when attendance at a Protestant service was prohibited. She reported how much she felt at home among Presbyterians now that she'd had a chance to do so. Gerry clearly approved of this sentiment, and noted that the leaders at the Second Vatican Council did not reaffirm the doctrine that most adult Catholics were taught in catechism, that 'the Holy Catholic Church is the One true Church of Christ'. He ended the column with the story of Paul Couturier, and printed his prayer for Christian unity. Gerry had to wait only one day for the first letter to come in from a reader. He was challenged on the point about the Catholic Church as the one true church of Christ. Gerry wrote back to thank the writer for finding a misprint in his article: his original manuscript had 'Roman Catholic Church' not 'Holy' as published. That, Gerry said, was the nuance he was trying to suggest, that there was a possibility of seeing the true church of Christ in larger terms than that of one denomination, however historic, large and universal.

Some of the stories Gerry was to relate in 'Communion' were very poignant. In August 1987, he wrote:

> There's a broken-hearted mother living in the Shankill whose son was killed by the IRA. To the Provos, the woman's son was just another legitimate target. The first time we met was just hours after the shooting. She threw her arms around me and said, 'I'm so glad you came.'
>
> I gave her a carving of Jesus crowned with thorns which a missionary friend brought me from Chile. It now hangs in her front room as a sign of our communion and in hope that God will bring good out of her suffering. One day recently she said to me: 'If only they had known him, they could never have killed him.' Could the tragedy of our divided society be described more poignantly than that?

In another column (October 1987) Gerry told of a Republican woman with a heart right with God and her neighbours, but also a heart badly broken.

> Some years ago her son who she dearly loved became in-volved in the military wing of the Republican movement. During all his life she had prayed that God would protect her son. Later, she found herself praying that other mothers' sons would be protected from her own dear one. Without considering the pain of it, she prayed that she herself might be the bereaved mother. Her son was dead four months when I met her. Our meeting was one of those encounters that make the north of Ireland a blessed place apart. She shared with me the heartbreak of her bereavement and said she felt utterly forsaken. She wondered if she had been right to pray as she did. Our pain-filled eyes met in silence. I could say nothing. People like that bring the heartbroken God of Calvary terrifyingly close to the rest of us.

After the infamous bomb in Enniskillen of Remembrance Day of 1987, the Catholic Cardinal Tomás Ó Fiaich announced that Mass would be said for the souls of those who had died in that tragedy. The Moderator of the PCI, Dr Robert Dickinson, called the Cardinal's remarks 'insensitive,' apparently since the IRA bomb had killed mostly Protestants. Gerry wrote in his December 1987 'Communion' column that he found that Moderator's comments might be construed as insensitive too. Gerry was sure that all Catholics had prayed for all the victims, not just those of their own denomination.

In another column (January 1988), Gerry told the story of Maria Gabriella. Born in Sardinia in 1914, she became a nun in the Cistercian order in 1937. At her monastery in Grottaferrata, she heard the abbess reading a letter to the community sent from Lyons by Fr Paul Couturier, mentioning those modern Christians, Protestants and Catholics, who had dedicated their lives for the unity of the church. She came to believe this was her calling too, and her elders also accepted that this was a genuine calling of the Holy Spirit. She was to live only another year, when tuberculosis took her life. In her personal effects was found her Bible, with chapter seventeen of John's gospel almost worn away with use. The verse she treasured most of all was John 17:14, 'For their sake I consecrate myself, that they also may be consecrated in truth.' Pope John Paul II declared her 'blessed' in 1983, saying that her life was a sign from God of what the ecumenical spirit should be like.

The 'Communion' of May 1988 must have seemed a bit strange to 'Couturier's' mostly Catholic readers. Gerry noted the up-coming anniversary of the conversion of John Wesley at Aldersgate Street Chapel, London, on 24 May 1738. Gerry quoted the most evocative words in Methodist memory, those of Wesley describing his conversion:

> In the evening I went unwillingly to a Society in Aldersgate Street. While the speaker was describing the change which God works in the heart through faith in Christ, I felt my heart strangely warmed. I felt I did trust in Christ alone for salvation; and an assurance was given me that He had taken away my sins, even mine, and saved me from the Law of Sin and Death.

It may well have been the first time that many of the readers of 'Communion' had heard such a conversion narrative, and it may have enabled them better to understand the experiences of their Protestant friends.

Gerry didn't always push the ecumenical agenda, but he seems to have taken what opportunities he could to gently mention a point of view that would nudge his readers a bit further along in inter-church contacts. For example, in his August 1988 column, he referred to 'icon places' as those venues that point us towards the vision of full communion with all Christians. He wrote of his recent visit to Ramleton in Co Donegal, which is known in Ireland as the birthplace of Francis Makemie in 1658. He became a Presbyterian minister and was the founder of the Presbyterian Church in British North America. A plaque on the meeting house where he worshipped as a boy reads in part, 'in the face of much opposition his stand for religious liberty won toleration for all'. Gerry thought the Presbyterian Meeting

House could be iconic, in that so many communities have claim on it: 'Geographically, the meeting house is in the Republic of Ireland; culturally is belongs to Ulster; historically it belongs to the Presbyterian tradition; internationally it is the root of American Presbyterianism; locally it is the centre of a scenic and historic town.'

Gerry's desire for Christian unity was the main impetus behind his writing the 'Communion' column. He was always unafraid to share the pain of exclusion caused by the divided church. Two examples of that pain will end this section on Reynolds' journalistic career. In April, 1989, he published a poem from a Protestant reader who had been in an ecumenical group of great closeness and unity, but who later was excluded from the Eucharist on a retreat weekend. The anguish is unashamed:

> This is My Beloved Son – hear Him.
> My Body is broken – share the bread!
> Do this in remembrance of me.
> I have broken down the wall of partition,
> I have overcome the barriers that divide,
> I have reconciled you to God.
> You are my body in the world.
> Be united in my love.
> Heal my broken Body.
> This is my desire.
> This is my command:
> Love one another as I have loved you.
> Then shall the world see,
> Then shall the world believe,
> Then shall my kingdom come.

Gerry's final column in the *Irish News* was published in June 1989. He reported on his own experience of being in the hospital for major cancer surgery. He spoke of the fellowship that developed between the patients in his ward, all Christians but drawn from the major denominations in Ireland. He was also grateful for the many people who had visited him, again, from the major denominations. He noticed, however, that while many priests and ministers came to visit some of the patients, none came to visit all of them, but rather ministering to 'their own'.

> It is a cause of great sorrow to me that there should be such distinctions in the ministry to the sick in one big ward. The doctors and nurses who treated us with so much kindness were Protestant and Catholic. They worked together as a team for all of us, making no distinctions, like Christ who made none when he said, 'I was sick and you visited me.' I will never again see the divisions of Protestant and Catholic in a hospital ward, but only Christ in each of his members and waiting to be visited.

Gerry was not to write the 'Communion' column again. After he came back from Jerusalem more than a year later, events had moved on, and he was not drawn to return to the newspaper to which he had promised two years. But, as said, many people in west Belfast still recall with pride and pleasure the column that had given those visions of grace to their lives.

Gerry Reynolds has another religious calling that we should note. As said above, while he was fully committed to the Fitzroy connection, he did not see that as negating another calling to link the people of Clonard with their Protestant neighbours across the divide on the Shankill Road. About the time of the IRA ceasefires in 1994, Gerry followed 'an inner prompting' to attend worship at a Protestant church on the other side of the 'peace line'. He was to return frequently thereafter, and he began to take Catholic members of the Cornerstone Community with him. By 1998, he was calling these visits 'The Shankill Pilgrimages' and by 2001, the informal name was 'Unity Pilgrimages', which went out from The Church of the Most Holy Redeemer. The point is fairly simple: when people worship together, the whole community benefits by the increase in understanding and trust. In the past eight years little groups have gone out from Clonard to worship at many Protestant churches in the area, including: The Church of Ireland parishes of St Columba, St Matthew and St Michael; the Presbyterian congregations at West Kirk, Ballygomartin Road, Shankill Road Mission and Nelson Memorial; the Methodist congregations in Woodvale, the Shankill Road and the Springfield Road. The total number of Catholic people involved averages about thirty in any year, with approximately eight on any given Sunday.

In the early days of the project, Gerry would always fix with the minister well beforehand the day on which it would be appropriate for the 'unity pilgrims' to come to join in the morning service. Now one of the pilgrims phones ahead a few days earlier to see if they would be welcome on a certain day. They gather at Clonard church about thirty minutes before the Protestant service is supposed to start. They centre themselves with the prayer of Jesus, 'Father, may they all be one,' because they see their pilgrimage that day as a little step towards that goal. The minister of the Protestant church invariably welcomes 'the friends from Clonard', which enables other visitors or irregular attendees to feel comfortable with Catholics in their midst. On a Sunday when a pilgrimage is planned, there is a special notice in the bulletin of the Church of the Most Holy Redeemer, and intentions of support are included in the Prayers of the Faithful during Mass. Those who have been 'unity pilgrims' are generally delighted with their experiences of sharing in the larger life of the church, and they are grateful for the simple ways in which these contacts may help to bring tolerance and understanding between the peoples of the Falls and the Shankill.

The final episode in the specifically religious activities of Gerry and Ken explores the significance of their joint participation in the Great Novena. It is one of the most popular and well-known religious activities at the Church of the Most Holy Redeemer. Its official name is 'The Perpetual Novena in Honour of Our Lady of Perpetual Help.' While it may sound like a historic Irish Catholic celebration, it was in fact brought to Belfast in 1943 by an American Redemptorist priest, Fr Matthew Meighan, who was a chaplain to the GIs stationed in Northern Ireland during the Second World War. He told his Redemptorist colleagues at Clonard of the successful novenas back in the United States. Fr Thomas Reagan, the Rector of Clonard at the time, obtained the necessary permissions and the novena was begun. While this highly successful set of events is surely a fully Catholic affair, it is also something of a community celebration, and Catholics feel comfortable inviting to these devotional services Protestant friends and relatives who might not wish to attend a traditional Mass. This openness to Protestant visitors is a matter of long-standing commitment by the priests and brothers of Clonard monastery, so the opportunity of the Great Novena to include non-Catholics is very welcome.

As the work of the Clonard-Fitzroy Fellowship was increasing in vigor in the 1980s, some people from the Fitzroy side began to attend the Great Novena with their Catholic friends from Clonard. In the 44th year of the novena in 1987, a Belfast newspaper, *The Newsletter*, wrote about the large numbers of people going to the novena that year – estimated at some 20,000 over the ten day period – and marvelled at the fact of Protestant participation. The rector in that year was Fr Seamus Enright who, when asked by the reporter how many Protestants attended, said he couldn't give a precise number, but that they all were very welcome. This report of Presbyterians at the Clonard novena provoked a letter to the newspaper by a self-described 'unashamed Protestant', who was outraged by Fitzroy Presbyterians in attendance, so much so that 'a challenge must go to the church's minister, Rev Ken Newell, as to whether he has been present at such novenas. If in fact he has, or have any of his church office bearers, I feel they must publicly declare themselves.' Ken replied to the newspaper that he had not been to the novena nor did he know what went on at one. But at the same time, he defended the reconciliatory work engaged in by himself and Fr Gerry Reynolds and by the Falls-Fitzroy Fellowship, as it was called then, a work fully acknowledged and supported by the Kirk Session of Fitzroy Presbyterian Church.

Twelve years were to make a big difference. By 1999, Ken not only had attended a Great Novena, he was the preacher on 24 June of that year. The Clonard website confirmed with pictures in colour what all in the Church of the Most Holy Redeemer saw: Ken dressed in his full Presbyterian regalia of collar and Geneva gown, and preaching to a packed house in the large sanctuary. Moreover, to the possible horror of some Protestants out in Belfast, but to the delight of the people in attendance, Ken preached on Mary. His announced title was 'Jesus and His Mother in the Gospels.' He acknowledged in the homily that Mary had been a divisive subject between Protestants and Catholics, but that today he was going to emphasise what they shared. Ken then gave a classic Presbyterian three-point sermon in which he affirmed that Mary's treasure was the love of the Holy Trinity: the mother of Jesus displays a willingness to listen to her Father's voice; the mother of Jesus displays a willingness to listen to her Son's teaching; the mother of Jesus displays a willingness to love people through the Spirit's inspiration. He concluded by asking the people in the church to love like Mary did, and to pray with him and respond. Three times Ken said 'Father, make me an expression of your love,' to which the people responded, 'Make me a channel of your peace.'

These various activities which we have discussed here were surely part of the larger vocation Gerry Reynolds and Ken Newell shared. They were not, as we have suggested, viewed by them as apart from their other activities, especially those particularly directed at politics and political actions. It is to them that we now turn.

CHAPTER FIVE

Engaging Politics

In an earlier chapter we discussed the interpretative problem of how religion and identity interacted differently with politics for most Protestants and Catholics. The latter see the Protestant-Orange state as the crux of Northern Ireland's problem, while the former tends to see the Catholic Church itself as the main problem. For the people of Ulster to engage in a civil discussion about politics will be all the more difficult because the two communities have typically not seen political ideas and actions in the same light.

Ken Newell and Gerry Reynolds are, as previously mentioned, people fully of their own communities. Even as much as they are friends and comrades in the search for peace and in the celebration of ecumenical grace, Gerry is as unembarrassed about being an Irish Nationalist as Ken is about being an Ulster Unionist. They could scarcely be credible in their own communities if it were otherwise. Having said that, though, one also recognises that Ken's and Gerry's overall strategy about politics was a shared one: they wanted to stop the violence and foster a process of forgiveness and reconciliation, both in religious and political terms, so that a normal society of democratic politics might be able to deal with whatever differences continued to exist between the two communities.

It is important to keep in mind that over the eighty-year existence of Northern Ireland, the people of the province have never known the working of normal democratic politics. Historically, the Catholic/Nationalist community has alleged that this lack obtained because of arrogant British imperialism and the unwillingness of Ulster Protestants to share power. The Protestant/

Unionist complaint always had been that democratic politics cannot work in a state who's nearest neighbour claims sovereignty over its own territory, or in a state in which a sizeable minority will not grant legitimacy to the existing political arrangements. So, because of these two sets of perceptions, the realities of politics have never approximated that of the two democracies – Britain and Ireland – most interested in a resolution.

When Ken and Gerry began their journey together in 1983, neither of them thought they would have any direct role in the development of a peace process. Indeed, some of their fellow clergy encouraged them, insofar as they wanted to work on reconciliation, to stay within the 'religious' realm and not get involved in the political dimension of the Troubles. Yet, both men were convinced that being faithful Christians did not allow them to do nothing or merely to defend their own community. Rather, they were willing to launch out into some deep water together, hoping with, and trusting in, the other friend.

The two peacemakers were quite honest about not really having a grand plan of action. Nevertheless, they believed that their vocation to peace work was a definite call of God. Therefore they never considered giving up. Even in the hard times of discouragement, when the way forward was not clear they would always keep trying. In all ways, they had each other for encouragement and reliability. In this regard, Gerry had an advantage over his ministerial friend, who had no other close colleague with whom to brainstorm, whereas Gerry had Fr Alec Reid right there with him at Clonard. We have mentioned Alec before, and later in this chapter we will make considerable reference to him. But enough for now to say that, in the developing friendship between Gerry and Ken, the priest's vision of a Christian democratic politics was very important to the minister's practical political thinking and acting.

The fluidity of events also militated against a strong and determined plan of political action, even if Gerry and Ken had one. It was not so much that they were controlled by events, but that as each new development materialised from a new direction, the two peacemakers rallied each other and their peoples in response. Their basic theological commitments were to be fleshed out in the developing political circumstances.

We have already discussed the clergy response to the violence of the mid-1980s in going to funerals and wakes, so there is no need to repeat that here. But mention of that suggests the degree to which Ken, Gerry and their colleagues Sam Burch and Alec Reid were willing to go in public involvement. It would be only a few small steps from that sort of engagement to speaking about, and becoming involved in, political action. Moreover, we have already seen that, in a situation like Northern Ireland, it is not easy to separate 'religious' and 'political' domains. Over the next pages we will first discuss the political ideas in the worlds of Reynolds and Newell. Then we will narrate their discussions with people some would call terrorists. We will conclude this chapter with a discussion of some events and hopes after the Good Friday Agreement in 1998.

The world of ideas will be our first concern, and it is best begun by discussing our main people, Ken and Gerry, followed by the thoughts of Dr George Dallas and then Fr Alec Reid. Ken's political thinking is not theoretical, but was developed in response to major events. A very important turning in his thinking was in response to the bombing at Enniskillen. On that Sunday morning – 8 November 1987 – crowds of people, mostly Protestants, gathered to participate in the day of Remembrance for war dead. Gordon Wilson, age 60, and his daughter, Marie, age 20, just home for the weekend from her nursing job in Belfast, stood with friends and neighbours. Without warning the IRA detonated a bomb containing 40 pounds of gelignite. It took down the wall of the community hall where the device had been hidden, and it killed outright the three couples standing near the Wilsons: William and Agnes Mullan, Kitchener and Jesse Johnston, Wesley and Bertha Armstrong. Gordon and Marie were buried in the rubble, unable to move. Many people later commented on the deeply affecting quality of Wilson's account on the BBC, describing how he and his daughter lay trapped in the debris, holding hands and talking. After a while, she said, 'Daddy, I love you very much,' and then she fell silent. Gordon Wilson survived but Marie did not. He deeply touched many people by giving the wonderful testimony, that he bore no ill-will to the murderers. His testimony is as moving now as it was then: 'I bear no ill will. That sort of talk is not going to bring her back to life. She was a great wee lassie ..., and she's dead. ... Please don't ask me for a purpose. I don't have an answer but I know there has to be a plan. If I did not think that, I would commit suicide. It is part of a greater plan, and God is good and we shall meet again.'

The next Sunday, 15 November 1987, Ken Newell changed the sermon he had intended to give at Fitzroy Church. This was a strategic decision, for not only was his own congregation to hear the sermon, but it was to be broadcast across the whole community on Radio Ulster. He now knew that his congregation – and, he hoped, the religious listeners of Ulster, and possibly the Republic too – would be ready to have contemporary politics engaged from the pulpit. For him, the Enniskillen tragedy changed everything, and it required from him and, he hoped, his congregation, a more direct response, to let the light of the gospel shine on political aspects of the Troubles.

Everyone in Fitzroy Church, and those listening across Ireland, expected Ken Newell to condemn the violence. He did, in no uncertain terms. In fact, he expressed his horror at the sight of the events on television. But then he moved to another angle of vision. He said it was relatively easy to condemn violence when it comes from the other side and is against our side. 'But when it comes from those whose political aspirations we have some sympathy with, it is amazing how in the back of our minds we find ways of condoning it, at least just a little, or so we think. The tragedy of Enniskillen must surely now have destroyed all such mental manoeuvring; all justifications for violence, all sympathy with those who act violently, from whatever source, died in the carnage around that War Memorial last Sunday.'

Instead of taking the easy and understandable route of simply blasting the IRA, Ken focused the light of scrutiny also on himself and on his fellow Protestants who were listening to the broadcast. It was not an easy issue to raise, the whole matter of the Protestant 'ascendancy' in Northern Ireland. It was precisely this set of attitudes and realities that Protestants must learn to repent of when remembering Enniskillen.

> After a past filled with centuries of violence and a present with thousands of broken hearts, I have a deep longing for peace; the Troubles have changed me, and Enniskillen has pushed that change further. I am a Protestant, but with no desire to see a Protestant Ascendancy; I am British in my political identity but with the highest regard for the richness of Irish heritage; I am a Presbyterian who enjoys deep and loving relationships with many of my Roman Catholic brothers and sisters in Christ. And after Enniskillen, the only ascendancy I am interested in is that of Christ's love and justice, and his reverence for life. In this I know I am not alone. But that can only be achieved if, after Enniskillen, we now – as one people – close our minds completely against the way of violence.

Ken surely must have startled some of the listeners on the BBC, perhaps more than his own people at Fitzroy who knew him better. The conclusion of the sermon pushed Protestants quite hard in terms of what they had to do if they were to remember Enniskillen rightly, that is, stopping simply pointing the finger of blame at others and finding the way in which each might contribute to the welfare of all. And Ken would not let his hearers be content with a safe but unengaged spirituality:

> While prayer is vitally important, it is no longer enough to pray without action; it is no longer enough to pray without repentance for the distances we have created among people in which suspicion and mistrust can grow; it is no longer enough to wait for God to send revival when what he clearly demands in scripture right now is the forging of new, healthy relationships and positive Christian attitudes without which this community cannot survive and without which we have no future.

Ken was aware, as he said in the sermon, that the Troubles had changed him, especially in respect of political consciousness. He was listening to the concerns of the Nationalist community though his contacts at Clonard and elsewhere, and had become aware of the thorough pattern of discrimination and hardship that the minority community had experienced. While he was aware that his own community might not appreciate it when he spoke up, he felt it was his duty tell the truth about some of the less acknowledged aspects of the realities of Northern Irish political life. At the meeting of the General Assembly of the Presbyterian Church of Ireland in June 1993, Ken substantially ruffled some feathers when in the course of debate he asserted that there had been 'long-term discrimination against Catholics in public sector employment' in Northern Ireland. He referred directly to the former Unionist Prime Minister, Sir Basil Brooke, to suggest that discrimination against Catholics was 'embedded in the Unionist political leadership'. Another delegate at the meeting interrupted Ken and challenged him on the accuracy of his comment about Brooke, to which Ken spiritedly replied: 'It is sin, it is evil, it is wrong. You need to stand up and say it.' When this was reported in the press, several people commented on Ken's statements. Most notable was praise from Oliver Kearney, chairman of the public advocacy group, Campaign for Economic Equality, who said it was a 'courageous and honourable declaration', which was the first time 'that a senior Presbyterian clergyman publicly acknowledged the endemic nature of anti-Catholic discrimination, and identified it as "evil and wrong".' What is clear in Ken Newell's engagement with political concerns, and equally clear in what we will say about Gerry Reynolds, is the desire to connect religious beliefs with social justice, but never associating that with a particular political movement or party.

Gerry, for his part, also spoke uncomfortable truths from the pulpit at Clonard's Church of the Most Holy Redeemer. His sermon of 17 August 1986 was memorable. Gerry was only three years at Clonard when an event took place virtually on the monastery's steps, and he believed that he must comment on it. But his way of doing so echoes Ken's desire to move beyond blame and towards what 'our' side can do to begin a peace process. We need to frame the event that caused Gerry to take his prophetic risk, and then comment on his words.

A murder had taken place on Dunmore Street, virtually in sight of Clonard, in the early hours of 15 August 1986. The IRA shot dead Paddy Murray, a member of the IRA who was allegedly a spy for the British security forces. The IRA later claimed responsibility for the execution of a so-called traitor, saying that it was convinced of Murray's guilt. There was no large funeral for Murray in his native Short Strand and not much comment in the Falls Road area. In circumstances like this, most ordinary people just keep their heads down and get on with life. But Gerry just could not accept that. He knew that 15 August was a near-sacred day for the people of the Falls Road who were gathered in the Church of the Most Holy Redeemer that morning. We recall that the fire-bombing in Bombay Street had re-started the Troubles on 12 August 1969, and that on the 15th, the Troubles claimed its first victim, Gerald McAuley, a 15-year old from Bombay Street, a member of the Fianna, the junior division of the Irish Republican Army. Young Gerald was hailed for trying to defend his own Catholic neighbourhood against violent intruders. In fact, that night marked the end of the old IRA and the birth of the Provisional wing of the IRA – what is commonly called the IRA today. They were a newer and more militant organisation, pledged never again to leave the people of embattled areas alone and undefended. One often hears that the Provos were born out of the ashes of Bombay Street and from the blood of Gerald McAuley.

It was therefore with great courage that Gerry began his sermon two days later:

> I have reflected much about this sermon. Before me were two options: to keep silent about the killing of Paddy Murray in Dunmore Street early on Friday morning, 15 August, the Feast of Our Lady's Assumption, and seventeen years since

the killing of Gerald McAuley, who was anointed by Fr Pat Egan as his soul went before his maker. There was no anointing for the body of Paddy Murray, nor priestly prayer at his passing.

For Gerry Reynolds to put together in one sentence the execution of a turncoat and the sainted memory of a near-iconic figure was to cause major dissonance in the minds of those at Mass that morning. But instead of keeping silent, and with the sermon hardly underway, Gerry led in prayer: for Paddy Murray, that God would have mercy on his soul; for the Murray family, that they might have the consolation of the Holy Spirit; for the IRA men who executed Paddy, that they might free their hearts from hatred for the British Army and the Royal Ulster Constabulary (RUC); for the members of the Army and the RUC, that they might acknowledge the wrongs they have done to the Nationalist community and seek forgiveness from those they have injured; for young people whose spirits have been coarsened by the Troubles that they might find the Holy Spirit in the community of Christ's disciples; for our political leaders that they might all come together to negotiate a just settlement to the Troubles.

Gerry went on in the sermon to request even more from his people. He announced that there would be a 24-hour period of silent prayer in the church, starting at 10:00 am on Monday, and going right through until the same hour on Tuesday morning. He spoke many words of encouragement so that people would come. He ended by asking his people to allow Mary to lead them in prayer, because there was no person more open to the Holy Spirit than she: 'Mary, Mother of Christ, faithful and gifted servant of the Holy Spirit, pray for us and gather us in prayer around your beloved son.' On the following day, for the time of silent prayer in the church, he prepared and left in the pews a sheet of prayers of the faithful in which he elaborated on the prayers he made in the Masses of the previous day.

A few years later, a sermon of Fr Gerry's returned to the subject of the political nature of prayer. He spoke of hearing an injunction from the Bible as if for the first time, of St Paul's recommendation that we should pray 'for rulers and those in authority, so that we may be able to live reverent lives in peace and quiet'. He realised that he must begin to pray for members of the British Government and of the British Army, even though he believed their presence among the Irish people was a main cause of his community's problem. Gerry said, 'I do not hate them or wish them evil, but there was often anger in me at their arrogance and their inability to understand us.' He acknowledged that it is natural to react in anger towards those who have wronged us and acted with prejudice towards us. But justifiable anger can be turned to good if channelled into the struggle for justice; yet anger could also turn to hate and that would lead to spiritual death. He ended the sermon with these words: 'Let us pray for our enemies and ask the Lord to direct our anger to the path of righteousness. Let us pray for the members of the British Government who govern us without understanding us, that God may relieve them of this burden. This is the gospel of the Lord.'

We will give one more example from Gerry of Christian political address. In a homily he gave at Clonard in 1998 he referred to the time, some twelve years earlier, when the first Anglo-Irish Agreement had been signed during the administration of Margaret Thatcher. All around the province one would have seen signs, reading 'Ulster Says No,' put up by Loyalists signalling their opposition to the arrangements provided for in the Agreement. When talking to boys in a class at St Gall's Primary School, near Clonard Monastery, Gerry mentioned his meetings with Protestant clergy, and he asked the students what they would want him to say to Protestants. The boys had various eleven-year-old suggestions. When all others had had their say, one boy spoke up with great insight: 'Ask them to say yes to us.' For Gerry, this was the insight that kept him going throughout the dark and difficult time of the late 1980s, that his vocation would be to encourage people of both traditions to say 'yes' to each other, and to find a political way forward to do so. Gerry saw anew the political meaning of the Magnificat:

His mercy is from age to age on those who fear him.
He puts forth his arm in strength and scatters the proud
    hearted.
He casts the mighty from their thrones and raises the lowly.
He fills the hungry with good things and sends the rich away
    empty.

We now move our concerns to Dr George Dallas, referred to above in the context of Fr Christy McCarthy and the beginning of the Clonard Bible studies. George Dallas was to make a great contribution in political thinking both in terms of his keen analysis and of his impact on many people. The best single source on Dallas is the booklet, *The Second Conversion of Dr George Dallas*, written and published privately by his friend, Dr Roddy Evans. In this source one can find an excellent summary of Dallas's contribution as well as the text of two key writings by Dallas. Evans's work will form the basis of our comments here.

Dr Dallas, though born in the Republic of Ireland, moved to Northern Ireland when his parents took teaching positions in Co Down, later moving to Co Antrim, where George finished secondary school. He attended Queen's University, and graduated with a medical degree in 1946. He was a dedicated Christian of Presbyterian origin and conviction who matured as a Christian citizen in the turbulent post-war years in Northern Ireland. Like many other thoughtful Christians in his time, whose lives had seen so much enmity, war and destruction, he was drawn to the Moral Re-Armament (MRA) movement. It was in dialogue with Irish Protestant friends, against the backdrop of the developing Troubles, that this thoughtful young physician began to develop his political philosophy.

One important distinction emerged in George's mind, that everyone in Ireland knew about, but few saw the significance of it. It is this: there was a three-fold nature of religious-cultural identity in Irish history: Catholic, Anglican and Dissenter; or, Gaelic, English and Scots-Irish. Since the mid-nineteenth century revivals, most people, including Presbyterians themselves, had lumped all Protestants into one camp, galvanised by political Unionism. But in reality, the true cruelty of English policy towards Ireland can be seen in the establishment of the Church of Ireland as the one and true religious and political identity. Catholics were a non-people, of course, but so were Presbyterians, who, in the eighteenth century could not participate in public life, and whose church could enjoy no recognised status. This is what drove so many of the latter to British North American and what gave them a political philosophy of democracy. So, while Presbyterian disability never approximated the thorough discrimination the English perpetrated against Catholics, Dallas developed a set of ideas in which Presbyterians might see themselves as truly an Irish people, not the half-Britons that the English had duped them into believing they were.

A very important step along the way for Dallas came through conversations with friends at his home. All of those who regularly met with the Presbyterian Dallas were themselves Church of Ireland communicants, all from the south of Ireland, and all Trinity College graduates. In dialogue with George, these southern Anglicans began to get a new vision of what England had done to others in Ireland, mainly to Catholics but also to Presbyterians. These four friends in due course would issue a public statement, published in *The Irish Times* to coincide with the meeting of the Anglican Church's General Synod in Dublin in May 1977. It reiterated the sad story of British interference and imperialism in Ireland, and it apologised for British actions in Ireland 'not in a spirit of breast-beating but in honesty and penitence'. While most of the apology was directed towards the Catholic people of Ireland, it also read in part: 'The Protestant Ascendancy that ruled in the Dublin Parliament was the Ascendancy of the Church of Ireland. So the penal laws were to some extent applied to Presbyterians also. They, like Catholics, could not hold office under the crown. They, like Catholics, were forced to pay tithes to help finance the Church of Ireland.' Roddy Evans, whose memoir of Dallas we rely on, was one of the authors of the 1977 statement, and Dr Evans later recalled that the writing and publishing of the statement was very important to George Dallas, and it assuaged a deep wound in his spirit.

In George Dallas's developing thinking, the way forward for northern Presbyterians was first to have Anglicans and Catholics see that the simplistic division of Catholics *v* Protestants as wrong; only then could the Presbyterian community move forward to see themselves as fully Irish, and then take their appropriate places in a United Ireland – even as Wolfe Tone and the United Irishmen of 1798 had hoped. This explains why George Dallas always referred to himself as a 'Northern Presbyterian', not as an Ulster Protestant.

One of the most remarkable friendships in George Dallas's life was to develop with Tom Hartley, a Sinn Féin member of the Belfast City Council. They met in the early 1980s and quickly came to trust each other. They remained good friends for the remainder of George's life. One absolutely vital point was to come out of the many conversations held between Hartley and Dallas, i.e., that the Sinn Féin man was to hear, almost for the first time, that there were Northern Presbyterians who would be essential to the success of a united Ireland once the main conflict with England had been settled. At the time, there was some stirring in the Republican movement to approach the Protestant or Unionist community. It was often dangerous to meet, and care had to be taken in finding safe and discreet places for discussions. On one occasion in 1994, when the whole political situation was very tense, Jim Lynn – a long-time friend of George's since the early days of the Clonard Bible studies – offered to help. Jim secured an excellent place to meet, through the good offices of Sr Marie Teresa Hoey, at the residence of the Franciscan Missionaries of Mary on the Glen Road in Belfast. We cannot know the exact ideas that were discussed at that and other meetings, but we can notice that in Tom Hartley's future public statements one can hear echoes of thoughts that reflect George Dallas's previous writing. It is a remarkable testimony both to Dallas and to Hartley's willingness to engage in creative new thinking. Their conversations contributed to Sinn Féin's new ways of proceeding towards the peace process.

We see this most strikingly in a key debate at the annual meeting (the Ard Fheis) of Sinn Féin in 1995. Tom Hartley took the floor to speak to a motion about possible future negotiations and discussion in which Sinn Féin might engage. Because of the consequent importance of Sinn Féin's political direction towards the peace process, it is important to hear two paragraphs of what Hartley had to say.

> This motion contains not just the view that dialogue between us and the Protestant community is crucial in today's political context, but also contains the dynamic for our party to update its attitude as a result of ongoing debates with northern Protestants. In the past our political view ran something like this: if you wish to dislodge northern Protestants from their political ties to the London government, then you must first remove the London government. It seems to me that while such a position is theoretically correct, as a political position it has tended to limit the political development of our views on northern Protestants. Should we be asking ourselves does this position lead us into a political *cul de sac* where our focus on dislodging the London government leads us to ignore the Protestant community?
>
> It seems to me that one of the possible consequences of the position I have just outlined is its potential to paralyse us. This is best summed up in the view that the Protestants will only change when they find themselves in a united Ireland, and that then, of course, they will suddenly come to their senses. In other words we do not need to do anything about the northern Protestants until we get the Brits out. Such a view, in my opinion, makes the Protestants of the north a non-people, to such an extent that they are robbed of their power to be a crucial component of the Irish conflict and indeed to be a crucial component in the search for a just and lasting settlement on this island.

Gerry Reynolds was later to tell me of his distinct impression that Sinn Féin's leaders experienced a substantial shift of consciousness along the lines suggested above. By the mid-1990s, it was politically permissible for Sinn Féin to speak positively about parts of the northern Protestant community, and not to reduce the world to a simple polarity of Republican/Catholics and

Unionist/Protestants. George Dallas's ideas and contacts were apparently important to that more nuanced political and cultural picture of society.

The final person we need to discuss in terms of ideas of a possible Christian politics is Fr Alec Reid, a colleague of Gerry Reynolds at Clonard. Fr Alec is a kind of shadowy figure because he wants it that way, believing that if he is to do his work of political reconciliation he must do it away from the public eye. Many journalists and scholars credit him with a major role in bringing together the various parties that made the peace process move towards Good Friday 1998. All the various books on the peace process herald the work of Fr Alec, but they piece together information from secondary sources, noting that he has never given a public interview nor gone on the record with any media people. In March 2003, by the intervention of Gerry Reynolds and Ken Newell, Alec agreed to talk with me for this book. It is a singular honour for which I am most grateful. However, I respect Alec's unique calling, and that his pledge not to speak specifically about his work has not been broken. Therefore, I can write only in general terms and about attitudes, not specifically about who was where and when and who said what to whom. His ideas are most insightful and his persistence in getting diverse people to talk together is legendary. We will want to probe his theological and political thinking, but before that we should try to get to know the man a bit.

Fr Alec was born and raised in a small town in Co Tipperary in the Republic of Ireland, where he grew up in the relative peace of the 1950s. He was ordained a priest in the Redemptorist order, and came to Clonard in 1961, where he was to remain for the next forty years. As he looked back over those years, he told me that it is sometimes worthwhile to remember how far we have all come together as Christian churches. When he was first in Belfast, the consequences for a lay Catholic attending a Protestant service was automatic excommunication. Even a priest could not lift the excommunication but only the bishop. That is some distance from Fr Gerry's 'unity pilgrims' whom we

discussed in the previous chapter! As to ecumenical activity between clergy (never laity), it was all very guarded, and kept on a
spiritual level. The Catholic leadership specifically proscribed
discussion of theological and political issues. The Charismatic
Renewal in the 1960s and thereafter broke down some of that
guardedness, but Alec was not very interested in what Fr
Christy was pursuing in his prayer meetings.

But the events of August 1969 were to change everything. In
Alec's mind, the fire bombing of Bombay Street on 12-15 August
1969, and the death of Gerald McAuley, marked the onset of the
public discussion about theological and political matters because they were right on Clonard's doorstep. Those horrible
days created a fear and anxiety among the people that broke for-
ever the rough consensus that had worked tolerably well along
the meeting points of the Shankill and Falls Roads and their
neighbourhoods. The interface between the two areas became
flashpoints for community uprisings and outrages against the
other side. On the weekend following the McAuley killing, the
army put up a temporary barricade that has since become the
formidable 'peace line' wall we discussed earlier. But in those
early days, one could walk across, or through, the barricades.
On 16 August 1969, a lay person at Clonard church observed
that a small bomb had been thrown over the barricade and had
exploded on the Protestant side. Fearing a new escalation of
fighting, he suggested to Alec that someone should go over to
the other side and talk with the people there about stopping the
violence, and that the majority on this side was still peacefully
disposed to the Protestants on the Shankill. That day Alec Reid
crossed over, beginning his long journey of crossing barriers
that would be so important and successful.

Alec knocked on the door of the first house on the Protestant
side, and a woman named Liz Wallace came to the door. Alec
said, 'I'm from the monastery. I'm here about the bomb yester-
day and to say that most of our community is sorry about it, and
we don't want an escalation of violence.' Liz Wallace invited
him in for tea, and thus began a friendship that would last until

Wallace's recent death. Over a cup of tea, Alec noticed that Liz had little plaques on the walls with sayings or scripture verses ('God answers prayer,' 'The Lord is my shepherd'). Alec began to see that in the homes of Protestants he found something in common. After Liz Wallace's house, Alec kept going on down the road. At the next home he was thoroughly tongue-lashed for the recent bomb, and then was asked kindly about the health of one of the Redemptorist brothers over at Clonard. At the next home there were few words, but lots of tears flowed among the choked-out feelings of 'thanks for coming over'. Alec later recalled that he was deeply moved by those initial encounters in those August visits when all the world of Clonard seemed to be on a knife-edge.

The friendships would deepen and stay with him. As he later visited with Liz Wallace he learned of a great Protestant custom of having a special Bible verse for one's life. Liz's was 'I lift up mine eyes unto the hills.' And that people have a favourite hymn; Liz chose 'When I Survey the Wondrous Cross.' Liz Wallace and the Protestant neighbours of Clonard were aware in a small way of Fr Alec's willingness to 'come over' the barricade. They could not have known that he was to cross over other barricades, ones that led him to discussions with Prime Ministers, archbishops, community and political leaders, and presidents of organisations some might call 'terrorist'. Through all the journeys to special places and among important and influential people, Alec Reid was sustained by the prayers of the ordinary people on both sides of the barricade he felt called to cross. Looking back now, he laughed deeply and with great affection at the memory of the late Liz Wallace's prayerful care for him during a lengthy illness, saying he was probably the only Catholic priest in Ireland who was told by a Protestant woman that every night she blew two kisses over the big wall – one for love and one for peace!

In the realm of political ideas, Gerry was later to comment that Alec was very interested in George Dallas's ideas about the contribution of northern Presbyterians to the future of Ireland.

This led Alec to a study of Presbyterianism, in which he was to admire its historical contribution to the development of democratic thought and action. He was aware, of course, that the democratic tendency had been hijacked by triumphalist Unionism in Northern Ireland. But, he thought, if there were more people who shared Dallas's view, then there could be a creative opening for dialogue between the two communities in Northern Ireland.

Alec has also done some of the hard thinking that has given political energy to his comrades, Gerry Reynolds and Ken Newell. There are only two known occasions when Alec went on the public record. In view of his enormous influence on events, it is worthwhile for us to pay close attention to what he wrote and said: in an article in *The Irish Times* in the mid-1980s and in a lecture at the inter-clergy meeting at St Clement's. In them we get insights into how clergy and people, like the Clonard-Fitzroy Fellowship, were able to conjoin the religious and political tracks toward reconciliation.

First, *The Irish Times* piece, in which Alec wrote:

> We must begin by lifting our eyes to a vision of the peace we want to create. That, in general, can only be a new political situation where the people of Ireland, in their Nationalist and Unionist traditions, are living together in friendship and mutual co-operation for the common good of all, and where the people of Ireland, and the people of Britain, are living together in the same way.
>
> How to make this vision a reality is, therefore, the great question on which all our peacemaking energies and abilities must focus. For those who believe in the Christian message of justice and love … this means that the principles of peace are essentially the principles which respect and correspond to the human dignity and human rights of all the people. … Rooted in the God-given dignity of the human person, these principles define the 'narrow road' which leads to political salvation. Any road defined by policies which lack the respect that is due to the dignity and the rights of people must, therefore, be seen as the 'broad road' which leads to political destruction. Here, those who believe in the Lord Jesus must

be prepared, like his first followers, to leave 'all things', all their partisan and sectarian attitudes, and follow him down the road of democratic justice and charity to whatever political destination it may lead.

It was this sort of straight-forward political theology that guided Alec to work secretly at bringing together the Nationalists and Republicans, especially John Hume of the moderate Social Democratic and Labour Party (SDLP) and Gerry Adams of Sinn Féin (SF), towards agreement on a democratic way forward, and then in helping to turn SF/IRA toward the peace process (of which more below). For now, though, let us continue to follow Alec's thinking as revealed in the only public lecture he is known to have given – at the Ninth Annual Evangelical-Roman Catholic Theological Conference at the St Clement's Centre. For Alec, the beginning point was an incarnational theology. He told his mixed audience of more that a hundred Protestant ministers and Catholic priests, that what he termed 'the serving Christian' must be a pastoral agent of the Holy Spirit 'in the midst of the conflict, in all its flesh and blood reality, in order to know the conflict from within and to see all the moral issues'. He reminded his audience at St Clement's that 'Jesus lived among us fully and unreservedly' and that 'he came to create a companionship between God and people, and among peoples'. For Reid, companionship is more than friendship or fellowship. Drawing upon linguistic roots, companions are people who eat bread together. Jesus used the table of food to foster this type of companionship, and he was willing to risk this companionship with all those willing to share his company. For Alec, 'the serving Christian [in a situation of conflict] must engage in sustained, direct dialogue with all participants. Thus, it is by listening in the midst of conflict that we hear the way forward, and we hear the words of Jesus from whoever speaks the words of peace.'

Alec Reid knew what it meant to be in the midst of conflict. From the mid-1980s onward he took a determined view never to condemn anyone, but to be available, as he said of Jesus, to all who would risk his companionship. Despite the fact that his spiritual leader, Cardinal Daly, was regularly condemning the violence, and specifically the IRA, Alec would not do so. He knew that on a given Sunday when he looked out on the congregation at The Church of the Most Holy Redeemer at Clonard he might see IRA people, some possibly on active service in the armed struggle and surely those who supported the armed struggle. He was absolutely determined to be their priest and not condemn them; but he was equally determined never to condone the violence and to try to find a way to end the killing. He was credible in the eyes of all not because he vacillated but because he saw his Christian role as the interpreter of each to all.

The credibility of Fr Alec can be seen in one of the most extraordinary scenes in the entire history of the Troubles. In March, 1988 there were a series of events that would, for a moment, catapult this quiet priest into the world spotlight. That month began with an 'active unit' of the IRA being spotted in Gibraltar. Although Mairéad Farrell, Danny McCann and Sean Savage were on an assignment of murder and mayhem among the British forces in Gibraltar, they were, in fact, unarmed at the moment that British forces in plain clothes shot, some would say murdered, them. (Three bodies received a total of 29 hits.) The three were brought back to Belfast, with Fr Alec accompanying the coffins on the road from Dublin. The three were given a solemn IRA funeral at Milltown cemetery in West Belfast, the near-sacred burial ground of the Republican movement. But, in the midst of the funeral, a loyalist gunman, Michael Stone, attacked the funeral party with guns and grenades, killing three people and injuring dozens more. Three days later, there was another funeral at the same West Belfast cemetery, this time for one of Stone's victims. The atmosphere was already supercharged with tension, both because of legitimate grief and because of Republican fears of another attack like Stone's. A bizarre event then occurred that broke the tension into blind fury and mob savagery. (An Army helicopter was hovering above, and the following scenes were captured on videotape.) A car drove into the funeral cortege. In it were two off-duty British soldiers, Derek Woods and David Howes, one showing the other, a recently-arrived recruit, around Belfast. The IRA escorts for the funeral cortege, fearing it was another attack, surrounded the car and encouraged the crowd to overwhelm it. The soldiers were dragged from the car, partially stripped and beaten. They were then driven away in a taxi to a vacant lot, where they were beaten again, this time quite severely. They were then shot and left to die. Someone in the crowd had the grace to call for a priest. Fr Alec was already in the funeral crowd nearby. Hearing the shooting he made his way towards the tragic ground. As journalists Eamon Mallie and David McKittrick recall the scene, Fr Alec 'knelt down in the dirt beside the spread-eagled, semi-naked body of one of the soldiers. Although he knew there was little or no hope, he bowed and, amid the mud and the blood, attempted to give him the kiss of life. … Fr Reid leaned down and pressed his mouth to that of the soldier; when he straightened up, after his hopeless effort, his lips had the soldier's blood on them.' A fellow-journalist, Mary Holland, also on the scene, later wrote: 'His courage and compassion redeemed us all. It sent one image of Ireland across the world that spoke human pity in the face of death rather than the savagery of the mob.' Mallie and McKittrick continue: 'In that ghastly tableau, Fr Reid was also the picture of helplessness, a living symbol of the impotence of organised religion and indeed of rational argument in the face of a merciless, determined gunman. Many would have given up; yet the same priest, spurred on by this awful experience, was able to play a hidden but vital part in bringing about the IRA cessation of violence in 1994.'

Alec Reid knew Ken Newell, of course, but the Presbyterian was more the friend of Alec's colleague, Gerry Reynolds. It was through Gerry that Alec was kept abreast of Ken's thinking. Alec also saw Ken occasionally when the later would visit Clonard with the Fellowship. So, in late 1989, when Alec's secret diplomacy within the Republican movement was beginning to bear fruit, he knew where to go, and to whom, when the time was right to bring Protestants into a wider dialogue.

Early in 1990, Gerry told Ken that there was an element within Sinn Féin who wanted to make contact with Protestant, Unionist people. Ken was asked if he would be interested in participating in talks. He agreed. This was a high-risk venture for Ken because he knew he might be meeting face to face with people who may have ordered the maiming of members of his own congregation or the killing of members of his own denomination. Further, it was politically risky because the official line from London and in Unionist circles in Ulster was that there could be no talks with Sinn Féin until its comrades in the IRA declared a ceasefire. Ken later disclosed that if his church people had known of his involvement in talks with Sinn Féin during 1990-93 (the IRA ceasefire did not come until 1994), 'I would have been in real trouble and would have basically been blown out of the water of my congregation and been demonised.' Ken took steps to protect himself in the potentially vulnerable position in which he found himself by inviting one of the senior Fitzroy elders, Denis Boyd, who was Clerk of Session, to participate in the dialogue with him. Denis later told me that he was not too hopeful or enthusiastic about this venture, and that he probably would not have done it without the leadership of Ken. But Denis also deeply wanted to see Fitzroy Church make what contribution it could. His participation not only brought a lay dimension to the heavily clerical discussions, but within days of the IRA ceasefire being announced, Ken and Denis together were able to break the news of their involvement to the Fitzroy elders before they all went into a Sunday Morning Communion. Denis and Ken were afraid that news of their involvement with Sinn Féin might have leaked to the press before the elders knew what they had been doing and why. Denis was the first to explain to the group of elders why he had become involved and then Ken took his turn. One by one the elders expressed their appreciation that they had taken these steps and gave them their unanimous support. It was a great relief to Ken and Denis that their colleagues were so positive; it was also a testimony to their qualities as spiritual leaders whose commitment to peace has created an ethos of such open-mindedness and practical Christianity within Fitzroy Church.

The talks with Sinn Féin were, of course, the most important, but there were other tracks of talks going on too, e.g., with the Protestant paramilitaries of the Ulster Defence Association (UDA). The religious actors in these talks varied, but there was a core group that almost always included Alec Reid, Gerry Reynolds, Ken Newell, Rev Sam Burch (a Methodist, and leader of the Cornerstone Community) and Denis Boyd. The first year of engagement with Sinn Féin was very difficult for Ken. He later recalled that he felt quite 'frosty' at first with the president of Sinn Féin, Gerry Adams. Ken later said that he probably 'sounded like a broken record as I repeated my viewpoint about ending the violence'. But Alec and Gerry encouraged their Protestant friends to keep at it. Gradually, each apparently began to understand more about the other than they had thought possible. Ken could now begin 'to listen to the pain on the Republican side, of people who grew up a mile and half from me, but in terms of their feelings, were on a different planet from me.' Gerry Reynolds may have seen all this a bit sooner than Ken, because he went into the talks quite sure that both sides had only a partial claim to truth, and that the role of the serving Christian was to affirm what one could in all participants' positions. In time, Ken did come to see that too. By the end of the first year, late 1990, Ken said, 'As I listened, I heard that they too had a compelling story of anger, injustice and suffering.' Denis Boyd was also impressed with the apparently genuine presentation of the Sinn Féin participants, especially Gerry Adams.

Meetings with Sinn Féin were frequently opened with prayer or a moment of quiet reflection, and sometimes with a Bible reading too. Ken vividly recalls the first meeting at Clonard with Gerry Adams and his colleagues. Gerry Reynolds opened his Bible and read from Psalm 85:8-13. The passage spoke powerfully to a situation dominated by violence, and it pointed the participants towards the peace and hope which faith in God makes possible and which human action makes real. Some phrases from the psalm began to etch their way into the consciousness of those present: 'I will hear what the Lord God has to say, a voice that speaks of peace, peace for his people and his friends and those who turn to him in their hearts.' Further in the passage we read Gerry's goal for the meeting: 'Mercy and faithfulness have met; justice and peace have embraced.' The meetings, led by Alec Reid, were mostly very business-like, in which, e.g., Sinn Féin might present a position paper, and another person, e.g., Ken Newell or Sam Burch, might make considered responses. On several occasions Ken evaluated key Sinn Féin position papers or speeches by Gerry Adams, identifying what he thought were blind-spots or misunderstandings of Unionist hopes and aspirations; but frequently he was heartened by increasingly flexible Republican perspectives and clear attempts to be more inclusive and less dismissive of Unionist values and rights.

While Ken Newell was grateful for the insights gained, by mid-1992 he reckoned that the talks were stalled and going nowhere positive, and that Sinn Féin was not prepared to budge. The IRA's campaign of violence was unabated, and its political wing was not willing to indicate much about stopping it. Reluctantly, Ken felt that, in the absence of Sinn Féin being willing to commit itself to a process of conflict resolution by first establishing a ceasefire, he should withdraw from further discussion. At this critical turning the two Clonard priests were an inestimable influence in two respects: they kept in contact with Sinn Féin, and they continued with Ken and the others in the parallel talks with Protestant paramilitaries, held at the Cornerstone Community, Fitzroy Church and at the Columbanus Community of Reconciliation.

Reid persisted with Gerry Adams and his colleagues in the Sinn Féin leadership, focusing on two points: that while the IRA could not be defeated militarily, neither was it going to drive Britain out of Ulster; that Sinn Féin was going to have to deal with Unionists in negotiations at the end of the day. In the light of these realities, Reid and Reynolds insisted, if Sinn Féin could not deal with the likes of their friends, Ken Newell, Denis Boyd

and Sam Burch, it could never deal with mainstream Northern
Irish Protestants. The exact workings of the collective mind of
Sinn Féin on this are not known, but the result is: in early 1993,
Gerry Adams asked Reid and Reynolds to come back to the dia-
logues with their Protestant friends. Alec later told me that he
was convinced that a major turning, long in the making, had
been made; that Sinn Féin had acknowledged that it was important for them to accept and respect Unionists, because their good
will was going to be needed if the overall goal of a democratic
society was to be achieved. Gerry had great but guarded hopes
for this new round of talks. Gerry Adams welcomed back Ken
and Denis, who noted immediately the change of mood, and
they appreciated very much the warmth of genuine friendship
and human concern they received from Adams. In Ken's own
words, and inimitable way, he later told me: 'The emotional
warmth of the meetings began melting the iceberg of traditional
responses. How do you destroy an iceberg? If you ram it, as in a
ship, it will sink you. But if you gently nudge it towards warmer
waters, it will eventually melt.'

Ken Newell and Alec Reid told me that the two sides found
new insights from the discussions. Gerry Adams asked Ken
about his allegiance, and Ken replied that his primary allegiance
was to the Lord Jesus Christ, 'and where he leads me politically I
will gladly go'. Furthermore, Ken insisted, if there was a united
Ireland tomorrow, that the agenda for him and Gerry Reynolds
would be the same, i.e., reconciliation between Protestants and
Catholics, Unionists and Nationalists. Adams was reportedly
impressed that a Presbyterian minister could actually envisage
the possibility of life in a united Ireland without it threatening
his faith or shaking his present political acceptance of the Union.
Further, Ken touched a responsive chord with the Sinn Féin
participants when he spoke of the deep sense in which Ireland
was 'home' for Presbyterians, and that they were neither just
British implants nor wanting to go home to England or Scotland.

On the other hand, what the Protestant participants heard
was that Sinn Féin's political philosophy had some essentially

Christian values embedded in it, such as their desire to promote the equality of all people and protect their human (and Ken would add, their God-given) rights. Adams and the Sinn Féin leaders insisted that such core beliefs needed to be promoted actively in Northern Ireland now, not postponed until a time of Irish unity in the distant future. The first step to implementing these values was to bring violence to an end as soon as possible and seek a democratic resolution of the conflict. Further, Ken, Denis and Sam heard that while it was ever important to Sinn Féin to envisage a united Ireland, it was no longer a precondition for political engagement with the Protestant people of Ulster, nor was a united Ireland to be imposed on them without consent.

The other strand of talks accelerated too. The same peace-makers were also meeting with designated members of the Ulster Democratic Party who spoke for the UDA. The then leader of the Columbanus Community of Reconciliation, Sr Roisin Hannaway, offered her building at 683 Antrim Road as a venue. She later told me that she did so in full awareness that she might be inviting an IRA attack if it became known that Ray Smallwood and Gary McMichael were frequenting the premises. She was understandably frightened by the prospect of violence, but with the encouragement of Alec, Gerry, Ken and Sam, (as well as her own community members and leadership, particularly by that tower of strength, Gemma Loughran), she welcomed the UDA to the house on the Antrim Road.

Meeting with Smallwood and McMichael was a first step. But through Alec Reid's network of personal contacts, another meeting was set up, this time with the actual commanders of the UDA, drawn from all over Ulster and brought to Belfast for a meeting at UDA headquarters on the Newtownards Road. This was the only time Ken Newell felt real fear. He was relaxed going to Clonard for talks with Sinn Féin and to Columbanus to meet with Smallwood. But at times of political tension he had received intimidating phones calls at home late at night from angry Protestants who felt threatened by his crossing the boundaries. He wondered if he attended this next meeting with Alec and Gerry, would the Loyalist paramilitaries perceive him as betraying the Unionist cause by his new relationships.

On the appointed evening the car containing Gerry, Alec and another friend travelled over to Fitzroy to pick up Ken at the side of the church. He said he had changed his mind about going and was genuinely frightened. He refused to get into the car. His friends pleaded with him and assured him that it would be okay. Some reminded him that 'if he was in for a penny, he was in for a pound' – that he had come this far and shouldn't stop now. Ken got into the car, still feeling tense and uncertain. Uncharacteristic of Ken, he remained silent during the formal introductions at the UDA headquarters where the commanders were introduced, not by their names, but by their place of residence in Ulster. By contrast, Alec Reid was calm and at home with them. He opened the conversation insisting that the members of his group were not emissaries from the Republicans but people in dialogue with Sinn Féin in the way they wanted to be in dialogue with the Ulster Defence Association. Alec and Gerry even managed to get a few smiles from the UDA men as they looked at the map of Ulster on the wall, and the priests asked why the other 26 counties of Ireland had drifted off into the middle of the Atlantic! Ken finally found his confidence and asked the UDA leaders why they had a strong dislike towards the Catholic Church and a deep hostility towards the Republic of Ireland. What, he asked, as Protestants, would they prefer the Catholic Church and the Republic of Ireland to become? How precisely would they like them to change? When the meeting was over Ken saw the UDA leaders in a new light. The dialogue had been honest and beneficial, but he was still glad to get home safely.

The pace towards peace quickened with the Downing Street Declaration in December 1993. New political possibilities opened up with the IRA ceasefire on 31 August 1994 and the ceasefire by the Combined Loyalist Military Command on 13 October of the same year. The ceasefires were never completely maintained but they created a new climate for political dialogue. One major tragedy and loss less than two months before the IRA ceasefire was the IRA assassination of Ray Smallwood outside his home in Lisburn, Co Antrim. Smallwood's past had included the attempted murder of the celebrated Nationalist Member of Parliament, Bernadette Devlin (McAliskey) in 1980. For this he received a lengthy jail sentence during which time he reflected deeply on the nature and resolution of the conflict. By 1993 he had emerged as the main political spokesman of the Ulster Democratic Party, the political wing of the UDA. His death caused great pain to Alec and Gerry and the other members of the group who had grown to respect his influence for peace. A strong bond had developed between them, and Smallwood's thoughts about peace had made a deep impression on them. The two priests went down to Lisburn on the night of Ray Smallwood's wake and were warmly welcomed by the mourners, particularly his sister Patricia. On the following day Sam Burch joined the two priests for the funeral at which Rev Roy Magee officiated. He had already laboured long with Ray Smallwood to move the UDA leadership towards the way of democratic resolution of the conflict.

Several weeks later, after the IRA ceasefire, when the whole clergy group went to meet Gary McMichael, Davy Adams and UDA leaders at the UDP offices in Lisburn, Ken Newell was aware that the latter were still grieving Ray Smallwood's death. He believed that it was right to acknowledge those feelings rather than go right into political discussions. He asked everyone in the room, about ten in all, to stand around the table for a moment of silence and prayer for Smallwood and his family. Ken recalls that 'of all the occasions when we met with paramilitaries, this was the most moving and miraculous'. Gerry recalls that it was Ken who invited him to lead the prayer. Gerry does not recall the exact words he said, but he is sure that the prayer arose out of the hurt, pain and anger of the occasion and the hope that faith in God gives. He said he had 'the sense that it was a very significant moment in all our lives; here was God acknowledged in the midst of life.' Whether or not Fr Gerry's prayer was the reason we do not know, but we do know that there was no UDA violent response to Smallwood's murder. The momentum towards the Loyalist ceasefire continued on course.

From 1994, when the first ceasefires were declared, to Good Friday 1998, when the Agreement was signed, the political process moved forward. That story has been told well and in detail elsewhere (e.g., McKittrick and Mallie, *The Fight for Peace in Northern Ireland*) so there is no need for us to repeat that here. But, for our purposes, one or two words need to be said. The cross-community group did not retire from activity when political leaders began to talk directly and openly. Be it recalled that in a democracy, political leaders can only go so far without taking their constituencies with them; conversely, if a constituency seeks change, political leaders must respond or lose their positions. So, even as one might laud the determined work of John Hume, David Trimble, Gerry Adams and George Mitchell on the ground, and the good support of Tony Blair, Bertie Ahern and Bill Clinton, if the political process is to succeed it needs broad and deep public support. As historian Scott Appleby has noted, 'top-down structural processes devised, negotiated and implemented in the political area are unlikely to succeed in the absence of parallel and co-ordinated cultural initiatives designed to build the social infrastructures of peace.' As in the picture of 'embrace' discussed in an earlier chapter, a community need not disown its entire particular past, but re-frame it towards mutual accommodation, forgiveness and reconciliation. As Appleby says well, 'lasting peace is impossible without a change of hearts and minds, without a new story to replace the old.'

In the immediate aftermath of the ceasefires of 1994, Dorothy Anderson, a member of the Presbyterian Church in Ireland and at that time an occasional visitor to Fitzroy, wrote a poem about the events and gave it to Ken. He later shared it with me as an example of the way ordinary people responded to the ceasefires.

The fact that it came from someone who knew of Fitzroy's work for peace was a massive encouragement and shows again how many Christian people within all the churches in Ireland supported the work of Ken and Gerry in their attempts to replace the old story with a new one.

> We rejoice that there is peace
> Throughout our land.
> In city, town and square
> No more bombings are heard there
> We rejoice that there is peace
> Throughout our land.
> We rejoice that there is peace
> Throughout our land.
> In field and country lane.
> No more fear of death and pain.
> We rejoice that there is peace
> Throughout our land.
>
> Our God has granted peace
> Throughout our land.
> He makes men see the fate
> The futility of hate.
> Our God has granted peace
> Throughout our land.
>
> But what about the hurt
> Throughout this land?
> Many grieve for loved ones gone
> Yet they know life must go on
> How will they deal with hurt
> Throughout this land?
> There is One who understands
> All who live in this land.
> Jesus knows the pain you feel.
> He can comfort. He can heal.
> Jesus is the answer
> For this land.

God can grant another peace
Throughout our land.
A peace of mind and heart
A completely brand new start
For all who come to him
Throughout our land.

Jesus came to set us free
Throughout this land.
He who was God's Son,
The pure and holy One,
Died for everyone of us
Throughout this land.

He who is the prince of peace
For every land
Bids us all be done with sin,
Ask his Spirit to come in.
Then the ceasefire will be held
Throughout our land.

Gerry Reynolds and Ken Newell are still involved in many
sorts of reconciliation activities. In November 1999 and in May
2000, for example, Ken and Gerry, with the help of ministerial
friends in the Presbyterian Church, the Church of Ireland, the
Catholic Church, the Methodist Church and the Life-Link
Group of New Evangelical Churches, organised a very large
group of Christian clergy and lay-leaders to come out into the
open in support of the flagging peace process. They published a
statement, 'Faith in a Brighter Future,' in three main newspapers, the *Belfast Telegraph*, the *Belfast Newsletter* and *The Irish
News*. Some 500 Protestant and Catholic clergy paid ten pounds
and signed their names to the following:

> We, the undersigned, are men and women committed to
> Jesus Christ, and wish to share our deep convictions at this
> time. We believe that in the providence of God, Protestants
> and Catholics, Unionist, Nationalists and others have been
> placed here together. For generations we have lived mainly
> in separation, rivalry and conflict. In these last few years the
> opportunity has been given to us to travel together in a new
> direction in order to create a healthier and more harmonious

society. Many of us have begun this journey. It has involved us in painful change but also in new challenges and enriching friendships. The political process is just one expression of this journey, but a vital one. The difficulties we face are real, but one way or another we have got to overcome them. There can be no turning back. This week is a significant moment. Our doubts and fears must not be allowed to strangle our vision. We are committed to continuing this journey towards the healing of our society.

When asked about this activity on a radio interview, Ken and Gerry told not only of the ad campaign, but of marching up to Stormont, the seat of government in suburban Belfast, to lobby the politicians further. Over a hundred clergy turned up to encourage their leaders to go forward. The clergy believed they were trying to do in church and society what the politicians were trying to do in government, i.e., to find the way forward to peace and reconciliation. When the interviewer asked how the politicians responded, Gerry and Ken observed that, without boasting, the clergy leadership was 'a serious and intellectually capable group' whose views the politicians seemed to value. Ken and Gerry thought they weren't seen as religious lightweights but as 'serious Christians committed to an inclusive society'.

The two friends have not retired from political engagement, as witness the ad campaigns and the lobbying, but leave the actual daily work of politics to elected officials of the various parties. The overall goal of Reynolds and Newell was forgiveness, reconciliation and healing in all areas of Ulster life. It was always out of this comprehensive 'religious' vision that their 'political' activities took place.

We conclude this chapter on the political engagement of Gerry Reynolds and Ken Newell with a document 'The Decalogue of Assisi' which Gerry gave me in Belfast. It discloses ten commitments made by delegates from all the world's religions who had been invited by Pope John Paul II to a meeting in Assisi, Italy, on 2 January 2002. Insofar as a contemporary political and social philosophy can be written on one sheet of paper, this would represent the thinking of Ken and Gerry, and the overall hope they have had for the people of Northern Ireland.

Decalogue of Assisi 2002
1. We commit ourselves to proclaiming our firm conviction that violence and terrorism are incompatible with the authentic spirit of religion, and, as we condemn every recourse to violence and war in the name of God or of religion, we commit ourselves to doing everything possible to eliminate the root causes of terrorism.
2. We commit ourselves to educating people to mutual respect and esteem, in order to help bring about a peaceful and fraternal co-existence between people of different ethnic groups, cultures and religions.
3. We commit ourselves to fostering the culture of dialogue, so that there will be an increase of understanding and mutual trust between individuals and among peoples, for these are the premises of authentic peace.
4. We commit ourselves to defending the right of everyone to live a decent life in accordance with their own cultural identity, and to form freely a family of his own.
5. We commit ourselves to frank and patient dialogue, refusing to consider our differences as an insurmountable barrier, but recognising instead that to encounter the diversity of others can become an opportunity for greater reciprocal understanding.
6. We commit ourselves to forgiving one another for past and present errors and prejudices, and to supporting one another in common effort both to overcome selfishness and arrogance, hatred and violence, and to learn from the past that peace without justice is no true peace.
7. We commit ourselves to speaking out for those who have no voice and to working effectively to change these situations, out of the conviction that no one can be happy alone.
8. We commit ourselves to taking up the cry of those who refuse to be resigned to violence and evil, and we desire to make every effort possible to offer the men and women of our time real hope for justice and peace.
9. We commit ourselves to encouraging all efforts to promote friendship between peoples, for we are convinced that, in the absence of solidarity and understanding between peoples,

technological progress exposes the world to a growing risk of destruction and death.

10. We commit ourselves to urging leaders of nations to make every effort to create and consolidate, on the national and international levels, a world of solidarity and peace based on justice.

CHAPTER SIX

An Unfinished Journey ... A Shining Moment

The main difficulty for the writer of a book about people like Gerry and Ken is how to end it. After all, their lives and work are ongoing. The two comrades have a history but they also have future. In the several senses of the word 'unfinished', their lives and what they want to accomplish are uncompleted. While they are near to retirement they nevertheless are still dynamically in-volved in their vocational situations. And while they are grate-ful to look back on the way they have been led, they are also very aware that, at the grassroots, Northern Ireland is only be-ginning to move towards right relationships in civic society and between the local congregations of the church. Everywhere the scars of a terrible past have yet to be dealt with and healed. This final chapter will focus on how they see the way forward. But as we do, we also glance back over our shoulders and we are aston-ished how far we have come. The wonder is not that Ken and Gerry have things left to do; the wonder is that they were able to accomplish so much in view of the 'troubled' context in which they worked. Their friendship is, to those who know them, a shining moment of what right relationships among Irish Christians might be.

The Good Friday Agreement in 1998 and the Pax Christi Award in 1999 were, in a way, markers that the prior work of Gerry Reynolds and Ken Newell had reached something of a conclusion. The first ushered Northern Ireland into a world in which politics had largely replaced violence. The second showed that groups like the Clonard-Fitzroy Fellowship might serve as some sort of model for others in the new Ireland. At the same time, however, Ken and Gerry did not see all this as a signal to ease up on their efforts. In fact, their vocation to peace and reconciliation was, they thought, all the more important once the shooting and bombing had largely stopped. With people now more able to focus on the future it became clear the peace builders also had to help others to deal with the memories of the hurts and the pain of the past. Both Gerry and Ken had always believed that the real work of social and religious reconciliation could only begin in earnest after the peace had come.

What strikes this observer is how much the force of inertia blocks reconciliation. Even if some individuals want to move forward, or have already done so, many others in their communities find the hand of custom quite heavy. Further, even with the best will in the world, there are still the flashpoints in which the old memories recur. For example, the determination of some members of the Orange Order to march through Catholic neighbourhoods triggers defensive responses from Republicans. In view of the Orangemen's presentation of themselves, one wonders if some people have learned very much from the long, bitter history of the Troubles. One Unionist political leader recently wrote Ken Newell, asking him to use his influence with the Catholic, Nationalist population to negotiate a settlement about future marches. The politician apparently could not fathom why Catholics should take such offence at what was called 'a walk home from church on a Sunday morning'. In fact, Protestant marches have traditionally been much more than a simple 'walk home', but were intended to be signs of the historic dominance of one group in society.

Beyond simple inertia and custom, there remains in the centres of opinion in both communities wariness about how much and to what extent one can really trust the other side. In fact, both Gerry and Ken are impressed with how much of their time is spent on explaining to his own side that it is acceptable, even desirable, to move towards, and with, the other community. In fact, a larger amount of their time than they had first imagined would be spent, as it were, standing at the places of engagement with the other side, but looking back to one's own side, assuring the doubters and questioners that this is all OK. In the spring of 2003, Ken was nominated for the post of Moderator of the Presbyterian Church in Ireland. In the polity of that church, every presbytery (diocese) gets one vote. Ken lost by the closest possible margin, 11 votes to 10. The next year, 2004, Ken was elected Moderator by a voted of 12 to 9. It perhaps suggests that his views on reconciliation and his well-publicised peacemaking activities have a wider support base in Christian circles than he – and we – had imagined. The Pax Christi award gave Gerry Reynolds and Ken Newell a higher public profile in Ireland, both north and south, than either of the two men had ever imagined or even hoped for. They consider themselves pastors in divisive circumstances in which they try to portray the gospel of *shalom*. But now they are listened to and respected on many levels because of the award. They continue to push the pace of change in Northern Ireland. Everyone may not always like what they do and say, but they are taking a large number of people with them on the journey of trust and peace.

Gerry's yearning for reconciliation at local level is rooted in his vision of the One Spirit at work in every congregation of the church. Since God gives the One Spirit to each local congregation – Catholic and Protestant – his constant prayer is that fidelity to the Spirit's leading may transform the relationships of the local congregations and enable the Roman Catholic and Protestant followers of Jesus in every place to become a community of friends. He longs to see each local congregation of the church make Paul Couturier's prayer its own:

> Lord Jesus,
> who on the eve of your death,
> prayed that all your disciples might be one,
> as you in the Father and the Father in you,
> make us feel intense sorrow
> over the infidelity of our disunity.
> Give us the honesty to recognise
> and the courage to reject,
> whatever indifference towards one another,
> or mutual distrust, or even enmity,

lie hidden within us.
Enable us to meet one another in you.
And let your prayer for the unity of Christians
be ever in our hearts and on our lips,
unity such as you desire and by the means that you will.
Make us find the way
that leads to unity in you,
who are perfect charity,
through being obedient to the Spirit of love and truth.
Amen.

Gerry has seen the Spirit at work in the simple encounters of ordinary people that accompany every visit made by the 'unity pilgrims' in the nearby Shankill area. Encouraged by that experience and by his long and ever-deepening friendship with the Fitzroy Presbyterians, he now writes confidently to ministers of Protestant congregations in the places around Northern Ireland where the Clonard Parish Mission team is working at any particular time. Having explained what the 'unity pilgrims' are and how they developed in West Belfast, his letter goes on:

> Our guiding principle in these simple visits has been that the command of Jesus, 'Love one another as I have loved you', applies to us not only as individuals but also as congregations of the church. Our motto and inspiration arises from 1 Corinthians 12:21: 'The eye cannot say to the hand, 'I have no need of you'; or again the head to the feet 'I have no need of you.' We are all disciples of Jesus. We need to look towards one another so that we may meet in him. We need to open our hearts to one another! We need to share our story and our gifts!'

In the letter and over the phone he explores with the ministers the possibility of a little group of the 'unity pilgrims' from Clonard and a few members of the local Catholic parish joining the Protestant congregation in their Morning Service at the time of the parish mission. While it may seem a small thing for people elsewhere, in Northern Ireland it has the potential to become the beginning of transformed relationships at the local level.

Gerry and Ken, as very close friends, have transcended their religious and political points of origin. They encourage others to think that a 'kingdom vision' does truly mean that we act differently towards and with each other. Their political goals of forgiveness and reconciliation were always an aspect of the larger transformation of the spirit they sought for Ireland. For them, and for many Christians they have touched, worship together is one of the activities that characterise the Christian life; redeemed people lead a Eucharistic life. Thus, when they attend worship at each other's churches, the pain of the separation between their traditions of faith is often very difficult to bear. Especially for people like Ken and Gerry, with a sacramental vision for worship and life, being separated at the communion table is particularly hard for the two comrades who have come so far together over so many years. Yet, even in this sort of pain, there are stories of grace to tell.

Gerry Reynolds has attended worship services at Fitzroy many times, and has been present when Holy Communion was served. He always had let the elements pass him, even though he felt the grace of the fellowship present in them. It deeply affected and troubled him, and he wept unashamedly many times. But, in November 1999, just two weeks before going down to Dublin to receive the Pax Christi award, he could no longer live with this deep contradiction in his life. He reckoned that his place in the fellowship of Fitzroy was so solid and his companionship with the people there so complete, that either he must participate in Holy Communion there or leave Fitzroy altogether. In mid-November 1999, he did partake. He told this story in a radio interview broadcast all over Ireland (on RTÉ, the Irish equivalent of the BBC) saying that his 'participation is for other theologians to sort out elsewhere, but it is where I am on the journey.' The interviewer asked Gerry if this is how and where he does his theology. Gerry agreed, contrasting 'the ecumenism of the battlefront and the ecumenism of the salon. For me not to partake two weeks ago would have been to make a mockery of the cross of Christ.' Gerry later recalled to me the full story of the impact on him of that morning in Fitzroy:

Fr Joe Tobin, our Superior General, and his assistant Fr Serafino Fiore were making a visitation in those days of the Irish Redemptorist province. Our Irish leadership asked me to arrange an ecumenical dimension to their visit to our community at Clonard. I got very short notice of this wish. So to offer our visitors an experience of worshipping with Presbyterians I asked Ken about bringing them to Morning Worship in Fitzroy on the Sunday of their time with us. It happened to be a Communion Service, one I will not forget. Ken asked Fr Joe Tobin to give his testimony during the service of what Jesus Christ means to him personally. The story of the centrality of Christ in his life had a profound impact on the Fitzroy congregation. During the celebration I was conscious both of brokenness and blessedness. Beyond the paralysis of our divisions, God's 'amazing grace' drew us deeply into that real communion which comes from 'above'. I was deeply aware of the Father in heaven opening his heart to us in the reconciliation which is in Christ Jesus and in the outpouring of the Holy Spirit which accompanies every Holy Communion. When in the course of the celebration Bill McReynolds offered me the sacramental tokens of that same 'amazing grace' I felt compelled to accept the gift after so many years of holding back. 'Caritas Christi urget nos.' That's what happened. I now see that morning as a significant stage in our ongoing and common discovery of the richness which is in Christ Jesus. Ken's generous welcome included an invitation from himself and Val for both our visitors, for the then Rector of Clonard, Fr Brendan O'Rourke and for myself, to join them and some of the congregation for a meal in the manse later in the day.

In the same RTÉ interview, Ken Newell also spoke of a similar story of pain and breakthrough. He told of having been a featured speaker along with other Protestant ministers at a large Catholic charismatic service in Dublin. Aware of the provisions of canon law, and not wanting to embarrass anyone, when the Eucharist part of the service came, he removed himself to the far side of the platform; he said 'so no one would see how lonely and isolated I felt'. He said he felt 'like it was a Christmas party and that I had been put outside in the snow'. Well, it seems there was a 'wee lady' there who went forward and received her communion bread but did not consume it. Instead, she walked around to where Ken was sitting (As Ken recalled: 'I'm 6'3", and sitting down, and she's 4'10' standing up, so we're eye to eye'). In a way that deeply moved Ken, she disclosed the grace of Christ to him.

In the interview on RTÉ in November 1999 Gerry said that it was for theologians to sort out where his journey with Fitzroy, his 'unity pilgrimage' with Ken, had led him. But he later offered his own share of insight to the working out of a pastoral theology for the pilgrimage when he spoke with Ken to the Fitzroy congregation on 2 November 2003 on 'the influence of friendship'. In the final question of the dialogue between them, Ken asked Gerry what he saw as the call and challenge facing them.

Gerry replied that only once in all of the nineteen years of joining the Fitzroy congregation at worship had he a sense of not being completely at home. That was at an ordination of elders in which he was keenly aware of the echoes of past polemics. 'All of us have to face up to that,' he said, 'and to our different understanding of what the ordained ministry is meant to be in the church. For that's what is blocking us from coming together in a common Eucharist.' In his own words:

> One aspect of the challenge from the Catholic side is to recognise the distinction between divine law – 'Love your enemies' – to which there is never an exception, and ecclesiastical law which permits the occasional exception. 'Lex positiva plerumque obligat – Positive law binds for the most part.' My generation of Catholics was reared on fidelity to the laws of the church and their exact observance in every situation. We grew up before the epoch-making decree on religious liberty of the Second Vatican Council. As we learnt our role and mission in the church, there was no place for the freedom of faith that might lead us sometimes to diverge from the letter of the law. We are in a new situation now but we have not grown accustomed to managing the tensions that can arise for us between the freedom of faith and fidelity to the law in particular situations.

Gerry then told the congregation, which included Clonard people from the Fellowship, that he would pray specially in the Holy Communion they were sharing 'for all those who have opposed us in our 'unity pilgrimage,' for all who have misrepresented us, hurt us or judged us as doing an evil thing.' It was getting harder for Gerry to say what he wanted to say. In the emotion of the moment, his voice almost left him and Ken placed his hand on Gerry's shoulder. But he went on to draw the attention of the whole congregation to what he called 'a terrible act in Christian history – the burning at the stake in Oxford in the 1550s of Bishops Cranmer, Latimer and Ridley because they refused to subscribe to a Catholic formulation of the doctrine of the Eucharist.' Sobbing as he spoke, Gerry asked pardon of God and of the Presbyterian congregation for 'this abomination which lies at the root of the terrible hatred for the Catholic Church which we see manifested in people like Ian Paisley. His Martyrs' Memorial Church stands in memory of the three bishops.'

There were many tears being shed as Gerry spoke as Catholics and Presbyterians confronted their terrible past. Ken had the last word. He just presented Gerry to the congregation saying 'This is my friend, Fr Gerry Reynolds.' The whole congregation acclaimed him as their friend too, in a spontaneous outburst of prolonged applause.

As theologian Miroslav Volf writes, 'In the Eucharistic feast we enact the memory of each other as those who are reconciled to God and to each other in Christ.' Another peacemaker in Belfast, and a good friend of Ken and Gerry, could not agree more; her agreement comes instead from the deep sense of loss about the way Catholics and Protestants are separated and segregated at the table. Sr Roisin Hannaway SSL, leader of the Columbanus Community for most of the 1990s, feels the pain very deeply both in excluding Protestants from her own church's Eucharist and from absenting herself from the invitation to the table of Protestant churches.

The situation angers me, makes me scream out inside. I complain to the Lord that it is dreadful, intolerable, unbearable and unChristian, that it is not what God desires. … It hurts people who want to love one another and to be at one. … There are days when my sense of justice is offended: I look around the [Columbanus] Community Chapel aware of the haves and the have-nots, those who are being fed and those who are hungry; and I wonder if we are not sometimes celebrating the Eucharist with bread taken from the poor.

On the Feast of Columbanus (29 November) in 1999, Gerry Reynolds was welcomed to the Columbanus Community on the Antrim Road by Roisin Hannaway. He gave the homily to the community on that day, in which he told the congregation of being profoundly moved by a celebration of the Eucharist he had attended in a congregation of the Church of Ireland. In respect of that experience he formulated three questions that pushed the argument about the Eucharist to a new level of intensity. His questions were these:

a) Does the Father in heaven give to them the True Manna, the living bread from heaven which we believe he gives us at the Eucharist? Or does he give them something less?

b) Does Jesus, our crucified and risen Saviour, become really present to give them the fruits of his passion as they celebrate the Holy Communion in memory of him? Or do they have to settle for something less?

c) Is the Holy Spirit poured out upon the bread and the cup of wine they drink to hallow them and make them the Body and Blood of Christ for their spiritual nourishment? Or do they invoke the Holy Spirit in vain?

Gerry concluded, 'When I lived in the Republic of Ireland, I never had to ask myself such questions. But now friendship and faith oblige me to face them.'

Gerry Reynolds is still well aware of the human and spiritual costs of incomplete communion, but he is delighted with the recent moves in his own church to study and address these questions. He recently shared with me an article written by the German Cardinal, Walter Kasper, 'Six Proposals for the Transitional Period of Real but Incomplete Communion.' That document, too long to be explicated here, has some important clues for our present concerns. The Cardinal encourages all ecumenical pilgrims not to give up on the ecumenical journey just because it is so difficult, or just because it is so painful to be separated from friends at the table. He suggests that people continue with 'an ecumenism of life,' in which the formally separated churches still do as much as they can together, such as clarifying doctrines, beliefs and practices in preparation for that day when full communion can come.

It is this sort of vision and articulation of Eucharistic grace that keep Ken Newell and Gerry Reynolds going, and their friendship so strong. Now approaching retirement, the two comrades look back with humble pride and satisfaction on the journey of friendship they have made. They are, however, still deeply troubled by the continuing scandal of the disunity of the churches. The process of societal forgiveness and reconciliation which has had such a good start in Northern Ireland still has some distance to go politically, but perhaps more so religiously. One wonders how much more can be done in other areas of society when the churches, long-dominant in Ulster life, are still insensitive and not reconciled in each other's ministries, and still allowing some of the faithful to continue to tell bad stories about other persons and denominations. In the view of Ken and Gerry, church people were important in the breakthrough that began the peace process; but unless church people enter into honest dialogue with one another at the local level they will impede the growth of peace. As the two friends said in another place, 'our doubts and fears must not be allowed to strangle our vision.'

The vision of two communities at peace with each other may be, in a comprehensive sense, some way off. But there are enough glimpses of justice and grace around Clonard and Fitzroy so that we never quite lose sight of the vision of *shalom*. Two examples from recent years will end our chapter.

On the evening of 2 August 2002, a remarkable event occurred in the Church of the Most Holy Redeemer at Clonard Monastery. The church was packed and the people were eager to hear the Harlem Gospel Choir which had been on tour in Ireland and the United Kingdom. The person welcoming the gathering to Clonard was Gerry Adams, President of Sinn Féin, in his capacity as President of 'Féile an Phobail', the West Belfast annual August Festival. After his own words, he welcomed to the stage and turned the microphone over to Ken Newell. Newell was asked to introduce the American choir, because he was well known to the people of Clonard, and had also recently served in the summer of 2001 for three months in the Presbyterian Church of Old Greenwich, Connecticut, close to New York, while on sabbatical.

Newell reminded the audience what a special day it had already been for the peace builders of Ulster. That afternoon he had joined thousands of other people of good will at a rally at City Hall to support the Lord Mayor's call that all paramilitary groups end their campaigns of intimidation and murder. The Mayor, Alex Maskey, believed to be a former IRA 'active service' person himself and now the first Sinn Féin Lord Mayor of Belfast, was in the audience at Clonard that night. Ken Newell acknowledged the Mayor and his wife, saying he hoped others would join him in praying for the 'First Citizens' of the city, that they might initiate many changes to bridge the chasm of distrust between the two communities. Ken further reminded the audience that there was much work to be done. For example, just two days earlier the Whitehouse Presbyterian Church near Belfast had been firebombed and burned to the ground. The minister, Rev Elizabeth Hughes, and her flock were devastated.

Back in Clonard's church, though, the evening ahead of them was one characterised by inclusion and acceptance, both in terms of who was there and of what was to be heard. Newell saw a deep significance for Northern Ireland in the songs of the African Americans whose forebears had walked in darkness but who now could nevertheless sing of hope and of the new day coming. Newell hoped others would also see the vision when 'all of us in this country will walk together as friends … and work together as partners'.

The other event occurred in Fitzroy Church on 12 December 2002, when Gerry Adams came to speak at an evening forum, called Zero28, led by an energetic young academic, Gareth Higgins. Inviting Gerry Adams to speak at Fitzroy Church is not quite as startling as it first might sound, because Fitzroy has a long tradition of inviting political leaders to speak on issues of broad public interest. Over the years Fitzroy has hosted such varied people as Unionist leaders (James Molyneux and Ken Maginnis) Loyalist activists (Gary McMichael) and Nationalist leaders (John Hume and Joe Hendron). But, in fact, Adams represented both a departure from established patterns and a sign of how far politics had 'normalised' since the Good Friday Agreement.

Adams was asked to address specifically the following questions: what do you want to say to the Unionist/Loyalist communities at this time; what do you want to hear from the Unionist/ Loyalists communities at this time? Every one in attendance at the meeting, and those reporting it for the media, were aware of the special quality of the evening, for here was an opposition political leader coming to a place where, fifteen years earlier, he never would have been welcomed, nor would he have had the political legitimacy to have been asked. Now with offices at Stormont and the leader of the largest Nationalist political party in Northern Ireland, Gerry Adams was a man one needed to reckon with. He spoke warmly about being glad to be at Fitzroy and with his friend Ken Newell, whom he had known for twelve years. He addressed many questions of Unionist concern, but one question most specifically: was Sinn Féin fully committed to peaceful politics, or was there a chance it might, along with its comrades in the IRA, return to violence? Adams reaffirmed what he had said elsewhere that Sinn Féin is totally and irrevocably committed to the peace process as outlined by the Good Friday Agreement. Adams admitted to some frustration that Sinn Féin has received very little credit in the Unionist community for its many contributions to the peace process and to the normal functioning of society under the Executive. Also, Adams wished the Unionist community would acknowledge more fully the large electoral base enjoyed by Sinn Féin. It is a large political party with substantial popular support, and the representatives of those people should be accorded the same respect as other parties. In the end, he gave a ringing endorsement of the need for all people to support the political process, and to support Sinn Féin's call for equality for all citizens. As to the latter, Adams said that democratic equality is not the possession of one political movement or one section of the populace, but a universal right meant for all, not a 'zero sum' game in which some people get more than others. The questions that followed were spirited and frank but, in the main, everyone was glad to see the operation of a 'normal' politics in Northern Ireland, in which an opposition leader was a welcomed guest in a church, not vilified and demonised even before the evening got started. While this was not necessarily bringing in the kingdom, the messy world of normal politics is, as Seamus Heaney remarked, preferable to the violent alternative very well known by Northern Irish people.

These sorts of experiences at Clonard and Fitzroy remind us of our two main people, Gerry and Ken, and of the remarkable ways in which they have been used in kingdom service. Also, the people of Clonard and Fitzroy told me that sometimes they have to pinch themselves to check whether they had been dreaming as they remember all the wonderful things that have gone on between the two churches. Twenty years ago, they say, who could have imagined that things would have evolved to the point where Ken could preach at Clonard and Gerry and Fr Joe Tobin, leader of the Redemptorist order throughout the world, preach at Fitzroy? Or who could have foreseen Fr Gerry, in his clerical garb, participating in a service at Fitzroy in which the baby of a 'mixed marriage' couple was baptised? I was in the congregation that day, and saw Gerry carry the baby up one of the aisles after baptism. The delight of the congregation was obvious, as we all were aware of the history being made. Or, most pointedly, who could have imagined Ken and Gerry, led by Fr Alec Reid, having a role in the discussions that would play a part in the eventual coming of the Good Friday Agreement? As I sat one evening in a meeting room in Clonard with members of the Clonard-Fitzroy Fellowship, I knew it was the same room in which the discussions had been held, and I could not help trying to imagine the transforming scene that had taken place there about a decade before.

Forgiveness, peace and reconciliation are still a work in progress in Northern Ireland, but one can look forward with some confidence. The Good Friday Agreement still enjoys majority support throughout Northern Ireland. And, as recently as April 2003, Fr Gerry Reynolds and Rev Ken Newell were on the radio again, pleading for listeners to give the various political parties all the support and trust they can. They reminded the audience how far the people in Northern Ireland had come since the darkest days of the Troubles, and how that was a cause for thanks. Listeners with long memories could also have given thanks for the long journey of grace and peace among the people of Northern Ireland by those special people, Gerry Reynolds and Ken Newell.

The special friendship between Ken and Gerry – and our telling about it – offer a kind of icon of grace, a charism for the church. The Pax Christi citation mentions their 'exemplary work at the grassroots level towards building the kingdom of the Prince of Peace.' In this instance, 'exemplary' emphasises a grace for others. It is not in simple, or false, self-effacement that Gerry and Ken, joining me in reflecting on their friendship, want to be seen as evidencing a reality in their friendship that is greater than the sum of the partners. That greater thing is a sign of God's reconciling power. It is, they believe, something gratuitous, something given from above. The reality of this grace beckons the friends onward in service; others, seeing this grace, will follow. In the end, the friendship is more than a personal grace. For those who can recognise it, it is a grace for the whole church. Of course they are vessels of clay, and all who know them know that too. But, their story points to a reality beyond them, to what is seen in them: no less than the reconciling power of the gospel. Therein lies its 'iconic' quality

Of course the overall vision of Ken and Gerry is unfinished business. We cannot realistically expect it to be otherwise. But we acknowledge that our previous life experiences did not prepare us to see this sort of friendship, nor to have expected the outcomes from it we have witnessed. This story might remind us of the lines from the old hymn: 'not with swords loud clashing nor roll of stirring drums, but with deeds of love and mercy the heavenly kingdom comes.' The deeds of love and mercy that have attended the lives of Gerry Reynolds and Ken Newell have been truly remarkable. As some people in Belfast said to me, we might well wonder if we will see their like again. But we do know this: in the mundane lives led by most of us, to know these men and their friendship is, for us, a bright and shining moment. In the words of the African American song that became the anthem of the struggle for civil and human rights around the world, hearing and reading about the friendship of Ken Newell and Gerry Reynolds, causes us to say anew that 'deep in our hearts we do believe that we shall overcome someday.'